HOLIDAY OF DARKNESS

A Psychologist's Personal Journey
Out of His Depression

HOLIDAY OF DARKNESS
A PSYCHOLOGIST'S PERSONAL JOURNEY
OUT OF HIS DEPRESSION

NORMAN S. ENDLER
Professor, Department of Psychology
York University
and
Consulting Psychologist, Department of Psychiatry
Toronto East General and Orthopaedic Hospital

A Wiley-Interscience Publication
John Wiley & Sons
New York . Chichester . Brisbane . Toronto . Singapore

Library of Congress Cataloging in Publication Data:

Endler, Norman Solomon, 1931–
    Holiday of darkness.
    " A Wiley-Interscience publication."
    1. Manic-depressive psychoses—Biography.
2. Affective disorders—Biography.   3. Depression,
Mental—Biography.   4. Endler, Norman Solomon,
1931–   5. Psychologists—Canada—Biography.
I. Title.
RC516.E53   616.89'5'00924   [B]   81-16179
ISBN 0-471-86250-9   AACR2

Printed in the United States of America

10 9 8 7 6 5 4 3 2 1

for Beatty . . . . .forever!

Foreword

Depression is a term with which we are all familiar. We use it often to describe a particular state of mood. In some individuals it is more than a transient mood or a temporary reaction to an unhappy event. It may come without apparent cause and render the individual incapable of functioning in his or her day-to-day life. The activities of normal living appear turned around and the affected individual not only lacks the wish to survive but he may actively seek ways to end his existence.

Such a condition affects as many as one hundred million people in the world according to the World Health Organization. We are also told that the incidence of depression appears to be increasing. Depression brings with it difficulties not only for the individual but for his family and for all those who come into contact with such an affected person.

The treatment of this disorder appears to be much more successful than is generally known. We have available treatment modalities that include antidepressants, psychotherapy, and electroconvulsive therapy. Many studies in the literature indicate that response to treatment is usually quite successful and that upward of 80 percent of the people who suffer from a depression are eminently treatable. This book is an account of one man's experience with depression as well as with the opposite mood state, mania. It is an attempt to give not only the patient's point of view but also the point of view of someone who is himself a member of the mental health profession.

The general public needs to know of the major recent advances in the understanding and treatment of depressive disorders. Attempts to convey such information by those of us actively involved in the field often fall flat or are regarded suspiciously as just so much mumbo-jumbo. We need to state that our field has been enriched with the results of well-documented research in biochemistry and neurophysiology. Psychiatrists and basic scientists are finding collaboration meaningful and mutually beneficial. To take an example, we now have what appears to be a fairly reliable neuroendocrinological test for depression. There is hope that this test may give us clues to the appropriate antidepressant to prescribe.

With all of this in mind, Dr. Endler's book will perform an important task not only to inform but to encourage the continuing productivity of research in this area.

EMMANUAL PERSAD, M.D.
Coordinator of Education and
Consultant, Affective Disorders Unit
Clarke Institute of Psychiatry

Toronto, Ontario, Canada
June 1981

On Sharing Darkness

This book describes one of the most harrowing afflictions to which human beings are heir. It is the journal of a man struggling in the grip of a severe depressive illness, of the onset and course of that illness, and of his ultimate triumph over it. The account is detailed and written with sincerity, yet laudably free of overdramatization, morbidity, or self-pity. As such, it is a most moving testimony. But it is more than that. It provides us with insights to the experience of a disorder that, directly or indirectly, affects most of us at some time. Interleaved with the story is a richly informative and sophisticated study of the affective disorders and their treatment.

This combination of personal saga and scientific exposition reflects nicely the qualities of the author, and the effectiveness of the book is a tribute to his vigor, resolution, and intellectual power. Norm Endler's personality shines throughout the book. He is an honest, pragmatic man, notably immune to pretentiousness, self-regard, or neurotic hangups. He is, in fact, an eminently stable person. His warmth, sociability, and good cheer account largely for the affection and respect with which he is regarded by his wide circle of friends. His life revolves around two axes, one of which is his family and friends; the other, his profession as a university teacher and researcher. He is an unusually gifted man whose superior intelligence is rendered productive by unflagging energy and a capacity for organization. It is not surprising that in his chosen area of academic expertise (personality/social psychology) he is a distinguished scholar with an international reputation.

Norm Endler's book contains an excellent discussion of the various diagnostic categories referred to as "depression," a term that we treat rather loosely. Some clinicians use it in its everyday lay sense as meaning unhappiness or sorrow, which are natural emotional responses to saddening experiences or profound disappointment. Certainly many cases of psychiatric depression are exaggerations of normal reactions. Technically speaking, however, "depression" is a term that derives from *depressione vitalis*—a lowering of the level of vital feelings. This "flattening of affect" involves a mood change that is qualitatively different from normal. Although patients often present mixed pictures, the phenomenological patterns of the two forms of depression are distinct.

Clinicians who overlook or deny the existence of the second form of depression will usually look for understandable connections between the patient's suffering and extrinsic events. They will interpret the suffering as resulting from environmental stresses with which the patient in question is unable to cope. From their point of view the most appropriate treatment is a psychological or psychoanalytic one. Clinicians who accept the differentiation between the two forms of depression believe that the second form springs from biochemical and nervous-system malfunctions as opposed to psychogenic conflict. (This is not to deny, of course, that the majority of mild depressions have a psychogenic origin or that psychological events may precipitate physical malfunctioning.) They therefore consider patients of the second type to be suffering from what is basically a physical illness that has psychological concomitants but is susceptible to various physical treatments.

Naturally enough, the first viewpoint is favored by many psychologists, particularly in North America. Norm Endler's discussion is particularly valuable, coming as it does from an expert witness who has not only had personal experience of the disorder but also has an outstanding academic reputation and is himself a qualified and experienced clinician. Before his illness he was a subscriber to the first viewpoint and an opponent of physical treatments of depressive illness. It is a mark of his honesty and open-mindedness that he is capable of a detached analysis of this thorny topic. Of particular social value are his reassurances regarding ECT, a treatment that is still regarded with almost superstitious fear and aversion by lay people and many psychologists.

The physically based (or "organic") types of depressive illness are conventionally categorized as "psychoses," as opposed to the psychogenic type, which is referred to as a "neurosis" or "abnormal psychogenic reaction." Norm Endler's determination to write about his illness reflects personal integrity and courage, for even in these supposedly enlightened days to be diagnosed as "psychotic" still carries unwelcome or even shameful connotations. Norm rightly deplores this widespread attitude, derived as it is from misunderstanding and outdated stereotyping. It is greatly to his credit that he has consistently put his beliefs into practice by refusing to avail himself of the cover of confidentiality. In making no bones about the nature of his illness he has consciously faced up to the risk of social stigmatization. In openly publishing his experiences he may help to counter misinformation and correct some social prejudice.

One further observation may be made here. Norm's account serves to remind us of the anxiety and stress caused by mental illness, not only to the sufferers themselves but to those around them. At the same time the efficacy of any treatment is dependent on the support, both during and after the illness, of the patient's family. As observed above, Norm Endler is a quintessential family man, and in his book he pays generous tribute to the unfailing courage, good sense, and understanding of his family. It could be said that the real hero of the book is his wife, Beatrice.

GRAHAM F. REED, PH.D.
Dean, Faculty of Graduate Studies
and Professor of Psychology
York University

Toronto, Ontario, Canada
June 1981

Preface

This book is about depression. More properly, it is the story of my depression, a bipolar affective disorder. The affective disorders are discussed from my perspective as a clinical psychologist, professor of psychology, active researcher, and patient. In the spring and summer of 1977, while chairman of the largest department of psychology in Canada, at York University, Toronto, and actively publishing and pursuing research, I experienced a depression—a "Holiday of Darkness." As a result of my roles as psychologist and patient, I have tried to interweave the personal and technical aspects of depression throughout the book.

Thus the symptoms, types, and theories of depression and manic-depression are discussed, as are the various forms of treatment. The primary forms of treatment are drugs, electroshock therapy (ECT), and psychotherapy, although there is evidence to suggest that psychotherapy is relatively ineffective in treating the bipolar and unipolar affective disorders; that is, those due primarily to biochemical factors. Therefore one chapter is devoted to psychopharmacology and one chapter to ECT. There is a frank discussion of ECT as an effective form of treatment, which includes a summary of the unwarranted biases against it. The role of the antidepressant drugs in treating depression are explained; that is, the psychopharmacological revolution in the treatment of the major affective disorders (bipolar and unipolar). Although ECT is probably the most effective method of treating depression, it is not used as frequently as drugs because of sociopolitical and practical factors. Psychotherapy may be a useful therapeutic supplement to ECT and the antidepressants. Lithium plays a useful role in treating the bipolar affective disorders and can serve as a prophylactic against their recurrence.

One chapter is devoted to general attitudes and the stigma that is still attached to mental illness in general and the affective disorders in particular. The history of depression and the evolution of the treatment of and attitudes toward this disease are described. In my role as patient I have attempted to recreate the suffering I experienced. I have also discussed the strong supportive role my family played during my illness and the reactions of my friends and colleagues—and I have indicated where I stand now. It should be noted that my illness was biochemically induced and not due to some childhood or other trauma.

I also tell how to recognize the symptoms of depression and what to do about them. It is hoped that this book will serve an educational and prophylactic function: educational in that you will learn something about depression, its antecedents, and treatment; prophylactic in the sense that if you think you have a depression you will seek the proper help immediately and avoid much anguish and suffering.

I wish to thank my wife Beatty and my son and daughter for their strong support throughout my illness and during the writing of this book. My wife read various drafts and made many useful suggestions, as did my children and my friends and colleagues Professors Morris Eagle, Raymond Fancher, Kathryn Koenig, and Marlene Scardamalia. Dr. Harvey Stancer also offered valuable comments. Dr. Emmanuel Persad not only read the first draft and made helpful comments but he also wrote the Foreword and made the initial suggestion that I write about my experience. Most important, he was the psychiatrist who treated me when I was ill, even though it must have tried his patience at times. Probably the two people who were most instrumental in my recovery were my wife Beatty and Dr. Persad. I should also like to thank my friend and colleague Professor Graham F. Reed, Dean of the Faculty of Graduate Studies at York University, for writing "On Sharing Darkness."

My former secretary Teresa Manini typed the manuscript from my inimitable (ugh!) handwriting. For decoding my hieroglyphics beyond the call of duty, and for making a number of valuable comments about the manuscript. I am extremely grateful and thankful.

The first draft of this book was written while I was on sabbatical at the Psychology Department, Stanford University, from the end of October 1979 until the end of April 1980. I wish to thank the Psychology Department in particular and the University in general for providing me with excellent facilities, and of course I wish to thank my home university, York University, for its assistance. After three weeks in Italy, primarily in Florence, with my wife in celebration of our twenty-fifth wedding anniversary, we returned to Toronto, where I completed the first revision on our anniversary, June 26, 1980. I revised the manuscript again in September 1980, in February 1981, and into its present form in April 1981. I went through this spring and summer without a recurrence of my depression. I feel fine both emotionally and physically.

NORMAN S. ENDLER

Toronto, Canada
December 1981

Contents

HOLIDAY OF DARKNESS

A Psychologist's Personal Journey
Out of His Depression

1

It Was the Best of Times

It was the summer of 1976, and it was the best of times. I was 45 and at the height of my career as a psychologist. My research record was fairly impressive and I was the chairman of the largest Department of Psychology in Canada, at York University. I was also consultant at the Clarke Institute of Psychiatry and the Toronto East General Hospital (Department of Psychiatry).

My wife and I had returned from two weeks in France. We had gone to Paris for the International Congress of Psychology, in July 1976, and before that had rented a car with some friends to tour Normandy and Brittany. We had a marvelous time traveling through the countryside and were invigorated by meeting old friends in Paris. We were also looking forward to taking a holiday with our children at the end of August. We were to drive to Quebec City and the Gaspé Peninsula in the Province of Quebec. All in all, it was a great summer.

The summer of 1976 was a restful one for me. I looked good, felt good, and was even beginning to lose some weight. The second edition of my *Contemporary Issues in Developmental Psychology* had been published in the spring. One book on personality with David Magnusson, my colleague from Sweden, had been published the winter before, and the second one with David was in press, to be published in 1977. David and I had also published a major article in the *Psychological Bulletin* in the spring of 1976. There were no major writing chores ahead for me in the near future, except for the renewal of my research grant on the effect of person by situation interactions on anxiety.

Therefore I could spend the summer in a relatively relaxing fashion: playing tennis, walking, vacationing, swimming, and watching the

1

Montreal Summer Olympics on TV. I was looking forward to the Rothmans Canadian Open Tennis Matches in mid-August, which for the first time were being held at the new Tennis Centre at York University. A number of us had bought a block of tickets for the whole series, which lasted about a week. Included in the group was Ann.

Although I had met Ann two years earlier, I had not had much contact with her. I had met her once or twice socially. Otherwise Ann did not exist in my psychological life. During the tennis tournament, in the course of general conversation, we discovered several common interests and a common background. We arranged to play tennis and found that we were fairly evenly matched.

Following the Canadian Open Tennis Tournament my family and I took off for a vacation in the Gaspé Peninsula, where we had a wonderful time. We discovered a magnificent motel in a provincial park near Percé Rock. In addition to having swimming and tennis facilities and being close to Percé Rock, the restaurant in the motel complex was a training school for students wishing to enter the hotel management and restaurant business. Not only was the service excellent but the meals were superb. The food certainly compared favorably with any served to my wife and me the month before in some fine restaurants in Paris.

Despite the fact that I was having a good time, I was preoccupied with Ann. I kept thinking about her and looking forward to playing tennis with her again on my return to Toronto. My wife and children and I spent the Labor Day weekend in Ottawa with my wife's sister and her family and we returned to Toronto midday on Labor Day Monday. Quite soon after I returned I again arranged to play tennis with Ann. In the course of time Ann and I became good friends, primarily as a function of our common background, interests, and a love of tennis.

Although I was chairman, I still found time to play tennis every few days. Tennis became my passion! Or perhaps that was merely a rationalization and I was looking for excuses to spend more time with Ann. We spent time discussing my Jewish background and upbringing in Montreal and her similar Jewish background and upbringing in Toronto, our mutual interests in psychology, books, music, and our mutual passion for tennis. I had grown up in Montreal and had attended Baron Byng High School (BBHS), the school made famous as Fletcher's Field High School in the novel *The Apprenticeship of Duddy Kravitz* by Mordecai Richler. Although BBHS was part of the Protestant School Board of Greater Montreal, its student body was 99.4 percent Jewish. In addition to Richler, its sons and daughters (gradu- ates) have gone on to do many wise and wonderful things in Canada, in the arts, the sciences, and in medicine. Harbord Collegiate, in Toronto, which Ann had attended, is considered the BBHS of Toronto and BBHS is considered the Harbord Collegiate of Montreal. Therefore Ann and I had much to share. Although I thought of Ann as a very close friend, there were no romantic or physical involvements.

At that time I had been married for more than 21 years. I was in my mid-40s, my wife was in her early 40s, and I had two teenage children, a son of 19 and a daughter of 15. My relationship with my wife was and is an idyllic one. We both grew up in Montreal and I had known her since she was 16. We had many interests in common. (Tennis was not one of them.) We had both been members of the same Zionist youth organization, both had spent a year in Israel (at different times), both enjoyed living in a large city with the ready availability of theaters, concerts, and good restaurants, and both enjoyed traveling and visiting interesting cities. My wife is an artist and a super wife and mother. She is also relaxed, easygoing, understanding, and undemanding. In fact, she never once questioned my relationship with Ann.

Why would I want to get intensely involved with another female (even on a nonromantic level) when I had such a satisfying relationship with my wife? Ann is extremely outgoing and ebullient, whereas my wife is more quiescent and reserved. Ann turns men on, and I guess I was ready to be turned on. But why by someone the same generation as my wife and myself? If this were primarily a mid-life crisis, it would be more likely that I would relate to a much younger woman, perhaps in her 20s. Why at this particular time in my life? I did not really question it seriously at the time. It was to some extent a matter of someone being there at the right time and the right place. It was more than that, however. In retrospect I realize that I was manifesting some of the symptoms of an illness: hypomania.

It's a long time from September to April, but not if you're having fun. During the 1976–1977 academic year I had much fun and enjoyment and was generally in good spirits. I enjoyed being Chairman of the Psychology Department at York; I enjoyed the graduate seminar on social influence processes that I was teaching; I enjoyed my research on anxiety; I enjoyed playing tennis three to five times a week; I enjoyed crosscountry skiing; I enjoyed going to plays and movies; enjoyed my new hi-fi stereo set; enjoyed being with my wife and enjoyed being with Ann. I was writing research papers, I was consulting at the Toronto East General Hospital, Department of Psychiatry, and at the Clarke Institute of Psychiatry, and I was "flitting" all over the place. Furthermore, between September and December 1976 I was able to lose all the weight I had planned to lose and boasted that I was down to what I weighed when I was 19. Should all this have been a premonition of a mid-life crisis? Not for me; I was too busy having fun.

Most of the time I was busy, busy, busy; taping records, playing tennis, skiing, writing manuscripts, talking to Ann, reading, going to movies, staying up late at night, waking up early in the morning, always on the go—busy, busy, busy. Furthermore, I was boasting about all the energy I had that enabled me to keep up this fast pace—something with which my wife did not sympathize. She was wondering why I was running around like "a chicken without a head" and asked me to slow down and take it easy. Ann, however, was sympathetic to my pace, probably because she had an abundance of energy and functioned at a rapid pace herself. Perhaps unconsciously I was attempting to compete with her or even to compete with my own youth. Instead of occasionally "idling" in neutral I was always in "overdrive."

In the middle of December I went to Miami Beach to participate in a symposium on Cross-Cultural Anxiety Research at the Interamerican Congress of Psychology. After three or four days I dashed back to Toronto, and after a week in Toronto my family and I took off for a five- or six-day vacation in New York. In between Miami Beach and New York City, Ann and I spent a fair amount of time together (tennis, lunch, movies) and I realized that I was becoming emotionally involved. As a rule I made a point of informing my wife when I was seeing Ann. Surprisingly, she never said anything directly to me about Ann or my relationship with her.

In addition to being preoccupied with Ann, I was also occupied with the Annual Meeting of the Ontario Psychological Association to be held at the Inn on the Park in Toronto in early February 1977. As cochairman of the program I was deeply engaged in the coordination of the program and with the arrangements for the invited speakers. As an index of my hypomanic activity, I arranged to introduce most of the invited speakers, a fact that I did not realize until later. Before the convention ended I flew off to South Padre Island, Texas (in the Gulf of Mexico) for a one-week vacation and tennis with my son. Busy! Busy! Busy!

Evidently during this period a number of friends told me I could never sit still long enough for them to have a conversation with me. Obviously I was unaware of it. Furthermore, my research assistant claimed that I never spent enough time with her discussing my anxiety research project and my secretary and administrative assistant commented that I no longer told them where I was going. I was playing tennis or squash or skiing or working in my faculty office rather than in the chairman's. The main point was that I was never stationary but always on the go. I went to sleep late and woke up early; I ate on the run. I fulfilled all my duties and obligations as chairman and carried out all my teaching assignments. I also fulfilled my fatherly and husbandly duties. However, my behavior was diffuse. In retrospect I realize that it was hypomanic. Furthermore, I was feeling "oh, so good."

When Ann returned from a trip at the end of March she indicated that she wanted to "wind down" our relationship. I must admit that I did not agree with her, for I saw nothing wrong in it because there had been no physical involvement. Ann seemed to be cold, distant, and bitchy. During that same week I was notified that my Anxiety Research Grant which I had held for more than 12 years was not being renewed. I felt twice rejected: first by Ann and then by The Canada Council.

The Rejections of April
and the Tensions of May

Passover and Good Friday both occurred during the first week in April 1977. So did the change in my relationship with Ann and the notification from The Canada Council regarding my research grant.

Toronto had been awarded a major league baseball franchise in the American League. Opening day for the Blue Jays was the day before Good Friday, Thursday, April 7, 1977, which was also the same day that my sex drive failed me—for the first time since puberty. I went to the opening baseball game with two of my colleagues and the mother of one of them. Although it was April it was snowing and cold. I was ready to leave after the first inning but my colleague's mother, who was 80 and an avid baseball fan, shamed us all into staying until the end of the fifth inning. I felt wet, cold, tense, tired, and unhappy. That evening I went out to dinner with a visiting psychologist and some of my friends from York University. We went to Fentons, a superb restaurant, but I was not at all enthusiastic about going. That should have been a warning to me that something was wrong.

After our conversation early in April, Ann and I agreed to see one another less frequently. Whereas in the past she had been warm and friendly, I now perceived her to be cold, hostile, and picky. I did not feel at ease with her but was probably still infatuated.

Toward mid-April I was having difficulty sleeping, my sex drive was completely gone, and my appetite was beginning to go. For the first time in my life I felt overwhelmed by my job and remarked to a number of people how difficult it was being chairman. I rationalized this and blamed it on external factors. The "Red Book," which was the report of the York University President's Commission on Goals and Objectives was published in mid-April. This report made many recommendations regarding changes in the Faculty of Arts and also suggested changes for the role of the Department of Psychology. Should Psychology be in Arts? Should it be in Science? Should it be a separate faculty? Although I set up a committee to look into it I felt inappropriately overwhelmed by the whole phenomenon.

At this stage the only thing that didn't suffer was my tennis. Every Saturday morning four of us played doubles, which I still enjoyed. During May, however, I became very tense and really had to concentrate on the game.

At work I was sullen and rarely spoke to or listened to anyone. If I asked my secretary a question I would leave before she could reply. I wandered in and out of my office—almost in a fog. I went home in the middle of the day. I wanted to be alone yet hated to be. At home, at the dinner table, I rarely spoke. I stopped reading the newspaper and watching television. This general behavior extended to the Department of Psychiatry at the Toronto East General Hospital, where I was consulting.

The surprising thing is that none of my colleagues at York or at the Toronto East General commented on my behavior. My secretary, my administrative assistant, and my research assistant at York all thought that I was angry with them. My secretary and administrative assistant did ask me, in May, what was wrong, but I ignored them. The secretaries and the screening clinic coordinator (who was a psychiatric nurse) at the hospital all asked me what was bothering me. My wife *told* me something was wrong and that I should see a doctor. I brushed her remarks aside and said that it would go away. Ann did not say a word. My close friends and colleagues, clinical psychologists, psychiatrists, social workers, and psychiatric nurses—all experts in the mental health field—did not say a word. Were they that unperceptive or were they afraid of intruding? Did they not care or were they too preoccupied with their own day-to-day business? My guess is that many did notice but were afraid to ask, lest they be mistaken. They didn't want to make fools of themselves. Perhaps the secretaries had more direct contact with me and the changes in my behavior were more noticeable to them than they were to my professional colleagues.

By the beginning of May I felt tense and queasy on the inside and jittery on the outside. I couldn't be still. I had difficulty eating, sleeping, reading, and concentrating. My sex life was zilch. I never smiled and rarely spoke. I imagine that I wasn't much fun to be with, yet I was too proud to seek help. Here I was, a clinical psychologist who was supposed to be helping others. How could I admit that I needed help myself? Back in August 1971, when my father died, I was sad and had some difficulty sleeping and eating but that disappeared after a few weeks. Surely my present feelings would also soon disappear. In 1971 they represented normal grief and bereavement. In 1977 they represented depression. But I would not admit it to myself.

I had been invited to deliver a major address at the North American Society for the Psychology of Sport and Physical Activity Annual Conference in Ithaca, New York, on May 23, 1977. Because it fell during the Queen Victoria Holiday weekend (a Canadian holiday) my family came down to Ithaca with me. Every little thing was becoming a monumental task. Everything was becoming a test of my personal competence. Despite my depression I was able to prepare my address (entitled "The interaction model of anxiety: some possible implications") during the latter part of April and the beginning of May. It took effort and energy, but I did it. (I also prepared two papers for the Canadian Psychological Association Annual Meeting in Vancouver in June 1977). We left Toronto for the conference in Ithaca by car on a sunny Saturday morning. There wasn't a cloud in the sky—a beautiful day. Everything was perfect, except that my apprehension was overwhelming me and the anticipation of driving was a great worry. I didn't know how I was going to drive. Of course, I didn't admit this to anyone in my family. Driving now became a test of competence. We started out toward Ithaca and crossed the border at Queenstown. I concentrated and the trip was uneventful. We stopped for gasoline and lunch on the New York Thruway between Buffalo and Rochester. After lunch my son, aged 20 at the time, asked if he could drive. With great relief I said "Sure." When we arrived on the campus of Ithaca College about five o'clock I was beginning to doubt myself, for every little thing had become a major production.

After obtaining the keys from the security guard we went over to the student family quarters where we would be staying. Our apartment had two levels, with a black steel spiral staircase leading up to the second floor. As I recall it, there was insufficient lighting and I found the place hot, oppressive, constraining, and restraining. My family thought it was quite nice. I hated the place and was anxious to get outside as soon as possible.

We went to a lovely place for dinner at a restaurant that was right on the waterfront. My son drove, for which I was again grateful. Ithaca is a hilly city with winding streets. I did not know how I could manage the car. After an excellent dinner we drove into downtown Ithaca and walked around a sidewalk mall. I was still nervous and tense and suggested that we go for a drive. We drove through the Cornell University campus, which is hilly and has woods right in the middle of it. We then came back to the apartment and prepared for bed. I felt very warm and could not fall asleep. I perspired most of the night (probably from anxiety), although nobody else in my family was uncomfortable. The next morning we all went out for brunch and I had strawberry crepes, something I usually enjoy a great deal. This time I had trouble finishing. I was so tense that I excused myself by saying I had to go to the bathroom. I went to the men's room and cried and cried!

After regaining my composure I rejoined my family. I managed to finish my brunch but didn't offer much in conversation. It was a beautiful, sunny day and we went for a short ride before returning to Ithaca College to register for the Sports Conference, after which we all took a drive into Ithaca to a section near the Cornell campus. We bought some bagels and ice cream (what an odd combination) and then walked across a bridge overlooking a gorge. We were told that each year a number of students commited suicide by jumping into the gorge, a remark that certainly didn't lift my spirits.

We then returned to our living quarters. My children left to play tennis, my wife stayed in and read, and I went to a reception for all the participants. Usually I enjoyed socializing but this time I just felt like leaving and did so after half an hour. Although I loved tennis, I did not feel like playing with my children. I returned to the apartment, picked up my family, and went out to dinner. We found a restaurant that was a converted railroad car. My family told me that the food was delicious, but I was so down in the dumps I didn't know what I was eating. After dinner we drove around the area and then decided to go to bed early. Once again I couldn't sleep.

The next morning, Monday, I got out of bed early, ready to give my talk. I walked over to the auditorium about nine o'clock. The conference was scheduled to begin at nine-thirty and I was to be the second speaker at eleven. It was extremely difficult for me to concentrate while the first speaker was presenting his paper. My throat was painfully dry and for the first time in my life I was anxious before a talk. I didn't know how I'd be able to present my paper. But I did. I discovered afterward that it was an excellent talk, although I did have to stop every few minutes to sip water because my throat was so dry. There was a lively discussion after the talk and everyone congratulated me on my performance. I felt terrible. I had lunch with some of the conference participants and escaped from them as soon as possible.

It was a sunny afternoon, in contrast to my blueness, and my family and I decided to go swimming. We drove to Buttermilk Falls, which is a few miles from Ithaca. My children climbed up the hill at the side of the falls and my wife and I sat at the bottom. It was another glorious day, but time seemed to move so very slowly, as it does when one is depressed. I felt listless and uncomfortable and was looking forward to leaving.

My children were having a wonderful time and could not understand why I wanted to go. Neither could my wife. Fortunately it got cool as the sun started to set and everyone agreed it was time. We went home and changed our clothes, went on to a nice French restaurant for dinner, and returned to the campus. My son and I then went to a party sponsored by the conference. Each of us had a few beers and talked to some people before returning to the apartment. Once again I couldn't sleep. The next morning, Tuesday, it was time to go back to Toronto. Although it was raining, I decided to drive. We planned to take two-lane roads rather than the superhighways. We stopped for lunch in Buffalo and then drove on to Toronto. Just on the outskirts there was a terrible traffic snarl, the result of a five- or six-car collision. I do not know how I made it into Toronto, but I did. Everything about the trip seemed opaque. Despite the beauty and grandeur of the scenery, despite being on a ''busman's'' holiday, despite the success of my speech, and despite having every opportunity to enjoy myself, I felt lousy. This helped me to decide that I was trying to cope with something beyond me. I needed help.

For the next few days there were special Senate Meetings to discuss the President's Report on Goals and Objectives. I sat through them in a fog. I played tennis with Ann but couldn't control my shots. During the last weekend in May I was at my wits' end. My wife insisted that I get some help and I replied that I would think about it seriously. Because I was having trouble with my tennis game, I finally acknowledged that there was something wrong with me. I was also teaching summer school in the evening and had difficulty concentrating on my lecturing.

Everything I did or tried to do sapped my strength. Everything became a monumental task and a test of personal competence, although I probably did things as well or almost as well as usual. Perhaps my standards were too high or more likely my judgment was off and I felt that I was not dealing efficiently with my life. The more I tried, the harder things became. I was very, very tired—emotionally drained.

My mood and behavior during April and especially May provide a lexicon for the basic symptoms of depression that I describe in chapter 2. I was anxious (e.g., dry throat, tense), uncertain, irritable, sad, upset, lacked confidence, cried, felt dejected, blue, shaky, and listless, could not eat, lost my sex drive, and was lethargic and sluggish, among other things. These symptoms are not unusual for a depressed person. What was unusual was that these things were happening to me and that I could not accept the fact that they were happening to me.

D-Day

On Wednesday, June 1, 1977, I decided at last that I would seek help. Because my son had an appointment with our general practitioner for a checkup on Thursday, I asked my wife to phone the doctor to see if he could see me afterward. While I was at York I couldn't sit still. I encountered my friend and colleague Morris and asked to speak to him.

I told him that I was feeling depressed and asked him if he could recommend someone I might see, discreetly. He said he would look into it and let me know. Morris and I decided to have lunch together. He told me that he had noticed that for a month or so my behavior had been different, but that he hadn't wanted to say anything because he was afraid of intruding. It was relaxing and soothing to talk to Morris, but I still couldn't eat my lunch.

I went to a meeting of the Social/Personality Area, but couldn't concentrate and left almost at once. Irwin, another of my colleagues, asked me to play tennis with him and I did. It was a chore for me to hit the ball and I had trouble focusing. My hands were literally shaking. I don't know how I did it, but I beat Irwin. Miracles do happen. After dinner at home I went back to York to teach my Introductory Psychology class. The lecture was on Personality, which is my major research interest. I don't know what I said, but I found out later that I had given an excellent lecture. I drove home feeling very tense and still do not know how I was able to drive. I was looking forward to seeing my doctor the next morning.

After tossing and turning I fell asleep at about one-thirty. About two o'clock the phone rang and my wife answered. I heard her say No! No! No! It turned out that her 53-year-old uncle had died suddenly of a heart attack. I remember saying No! No! No! I'll never make it! I can't cope! I can't handle it! I lay sleepless the rest of the night.

I had gone from being a winner to feeling like a loser. Depression had turned it around for me. From being on top of the world in the fall, I suddenly felt useless, inept, sad, and anxious in the spring. My D-Day had arrived! Where would I go from there?

2
A Time to Win and a Time to Lose

Manic-Depression

Manic-depression is an illness that strikes millions of people in North America. Not only does it create havoc, frustration, and despair for those afflicted with it but their relatives and peers also suffer as a consequence. Although it is a recurring illness, it is eminently treatable and hardly anyone has died from manic-depression, per se. It can be fatal, however, by exhaustion and dehydration and it can lead to suicide.

At this point let me discuss briefly some of the clinical symptoms of this mood or affective disorder and then follow with my encounter with my "holiday of darkness." A number of symptoms are characteristic of the manic phase of manic-depressive disorders and not every patient manifests *all* of them. Similarly, not all patients manifest all the symptoms that are characteristic of the depressive phase.

The affective disorders include a primary and a secondary group. The two types of primary affective disorder are bipolar (manic-depressive) and unipolar (depressive). (A third category—manic—has also been proposed, but it is not prevalent. A former distinction, used for many years but now in "official" disfavor, is that between reactive depression, or depression due to external stress and loss, and endogenous depression, or depression due to unknown internal factors.) In manic-depressive disorders there is mania and, most frequently but not necessarily always, depression. In unipolar disorders there is only depression. Both unipolar and bipolar disorders can be recurring and episodic.

12

Depression and mania are primarily disturbances of mood, although there are also disturbances in attention, thought, motor activity, and sleeping and eating habits. In the manic phase a person may be over confident, elated, argumentative, angry, and irritable. Speech is usually rapid and incessant, grandiose plans are made that are unrealistic, changes from one topic to another are frequent, and poor judgement is often shown. An increase in motor activity sometimes reaches the point of meaningless and purposeless hyperactivity. Distractibility is prevalent, focusing on a task may be difficult, and sleep as a rule is only fitful. In hypomania these symptoms are subdued, and there is no loss of touch with reality. All of us show some hypomanic symptoms at some time in our lives. It is when they become the core of our behavior that they are considered pathological.

The symptoms of depression include a sad, dejected, and apathetic mood, a feeling of hopelessness, a negative self-concept and low self-esteem, indecisiveness, loss of appetite, loss of sexual desire, sleeplessness, loss of energy and interest, lethargy and agitation, guilt, lack of concentration, and often recurrent thoughts of suicide and death. Here, too, all of us show depressive symptoms from time to time, but they do not persist and are not the core of our existence. The presence of at least four of these symptoms, lasting for more than a week, would strongly suggest a depressive illness. Run, don't walk to your doctor!

Secondary depression exists not only when these symptoms occur but also when other disorders (e.g., neuroses, schizophrenia) are primary and/or in circumstances in which they are reactions to incapacitating physical illness, to a sickness that is threatening to life, or to the death, loss, or separation of someone very close. The biological, biochemical, and genetic picture is quite different for the primary affective disorders than for the secondary.

The depressive phase is more disturbing and much easier to recognize than the manic. Depression used to be called melancholia. The term *melancholia* is derived from the Greek words *melan,* meaning *black,* and *choler,* meaning *bile.* Hippocrates, the Greek physician, in the fourth century B.C., suggested that melancholia was due to an excess of black bile (other emotional states were related to other bodily humors). Artaeus, the Cappadocian physician, in the second century A.D., was the first to point to the relationship between melancholia and the opposite emotional state of mania. The existence of depression has been known from biblical times, from the reigns of Nebuchadnezzar (king of the Babylonians, 2500 years ago), Saul (king of the Hebrews), and Herod (a Roman king).

Depression Through History

Depression is not just for our age nor is it reserved for the mighty and famous. It has a long history in both simple and complex cultures. It is part of human nature and is not merely a spin-off due to the anxieties created by modern society. It is the common cold of the emotional disorders but obviously causes more anguish and takes longer to alleviate.

The affective disorders have a long history but a short past. In ancient days depression was "explained" in terms of religion or magic; for example, the Babylonians believed that demons had somehow taken possession of the affected person and this brought about the depressed symptoms. The Hebrews, on the other hand, believed that depression was brought on by human guilt and divine retribution. Hippocrates believed that mental illness was due to humidity of the brain, and Aretaeus of Cappadocia proposed that melancholy was composed of two separate illnesses with common symptoms. The first was basically organic and independent of external factors. The second was due to psychological factors in that emotional stress induces depressive reactions. This distinction is analogous to a contemporary one, discussed above, between *endogenous* and *reactive* depression.

In medieval times, however, there was a return to a more religious and demonic explanation of depression. During the Middle Ages depressives were believed to be bewitched and sometimes the witches themselves. Even Martin Luther, in the sixteenth century, called melancholy the work of the devil. Psychiatric interpretations and treatment of depression was begun effectively in 1793 by Philippe Pinel, a French physician. Although Pinel is remembered primarily for removing the chains from the inmates at Bicêtre in 1793 and at La Salpêtriére in Paris in 1795 and for revolutionizing the treatment of mental illness, he also had a theory about melancholy. (In fact, Jean Bapstiste Pussin, "governor of the insane," first at L'Hospice de Bicêtre and then at La Salpêtriére, initiated the removal of the chains and other reforms, but Pinel is usually given the credit for these acts of humanity.) Philippe Pinel postulated that there were two facets to melancholy. At the base was a mental anomaly, but superimposed were severe physical symptoms. Because there were two facets, Pinel recommended two types of treatment for melancholy: *remèdes simples* for physical problems and *traitement moral* for the mental. Although *traitement moral* was not modern psychoanalysis, it did attempt to treat melancholy by having the patient "talk out" the problems. *Remèdes simples* included some early forms of "shock" treatment such as ice-cold showers, whippings with stinging nettles, and other methods of torture.

The next major "advance" in depression was introduced by Freud, about 1900. Freud believed that depression was related to some childhood trauma (e.g., a loss), combined with a predisposed personality. According to Freudian theory, depression is a function of guilt and hostility turned toward the self. Although Freud's theory, which holds only for reactive depression, emphasized the experiential causative factors of depression, he did believe that ultimately an organic and/or biochemical basis for the affective disorders would be found. See Chapter 10, p. 113, for further details.

The biochemical revolution, with respect to the explanation and treatment of the affective disorders, began by chance more than by design in the 1950s. But more about that later. It is enough to say at this time that one index of the arrival of the biochemical and psychopharmacological revolution in mental illness is that both *Time* and *Newsweek* had cover stories on this issue in 1979.

In addition to the influence of Pinel, Freud, and psychopharmacology on mental health, behavior modification techniques have had a significant impact on the treatment of emotional problems and on the field of psychology. In general, however, these behavior modification techniques do not lend themselves readily to the treatment of bipolar and unipolar affective disorders. Therefore we have not focused on this approach.

A Who's Who of Melancholics

The affective disorders have troubled people from all walks of life. Perhaps this "Who's Who" of depressives will indicate that just because the victims are depressed does not mean that they are not functioning—at least at some level. We may feel uncomfortable in the presence of depressives, but this does not mean that they are nonentities or degenerate. The illness is cyclical and occurs in waves, and for manic-depressives we get swings from highs to lows and from lows to highs. This survey may also suggest the possibility that for some people the swings facilitate productivity. It may also be possible that some people are important because they have accomplished something despite their depression. Perhaps, at least for some depressives, it is the very fact that they set standards so high that they cannot achieve all they wish. This perceived failure makes them especially vulnerable to depression.

A number of famous people, as indicated earlier, have suffered from the affective disorders or, as the psychiatrist Ronald Fieve refers to them, mood swings. In certain periods in history and in certain countries the affective disorders have been more prevalent and in other periods and countries they have been less so. The reign of England's Queen Elizabeth in the sixteenth century is often referred to as the age of melancholy. A classic work on the topic, *The Anatomy of Melancholy,* was written in 1621 by Robert Burton, a contemporary of Shakespeare. Burton, a quiet, shy Anglican clergyman and librarian, was himself a depressive. It took him more than 20 years to write his 500,000-word classic. There were five subsequent editions to this tome. Robert Burton discusses the relationship between madness and creativity and suggests that the *vile rock of melancholy* is one of the milder, but frequent, forms of creativity.

Elizabeth I was born in 1533 and reigned over England and Ireland from 1558 to 1603. Her era, which is known as the Elizabethan Age, was characterized by, among other things, a fair amount of melancholy. In some ways the last half of the sixteenth century was similar to the present. During Elizabeth's reign England developed from a comparatively minor nation into a world power. Social upheaval, questioning of values and morals, and role changes were concomitant with this rise in power, but like today there was uncertainty about the future and a rich literature with melancholy overtures. It was also the age of Shakespeare. Melancholy is dramatically illustrated in *Hamlet.*

During the nineteenth century the writings of Fyodor Dostoyevsky, Edgar Allan Poe, and Nathaniel Hawthorne brilliantly expressed the nature of melancholy and emphasized their own inner anguish. For

Edgar Allan Poe melancholy was the source of his demise. He finally ruined himself with opium and alcohol. George III, who reigned during the eighteenth century, was a manic-depressive.

Until the end of the nineteenth century madness was considered related to genius, probably because of the impetus of Romanticism. The greatest thrust for the notion of mad genius came from Goethe's book *The Sorrows of Young Werther*, published in 1774. Modeling themselves on the young genius–flawed hero, a number of young men throughout Europe committed suicide and Goethe's novel was banned. During this period it was considered the "in thing" for every romantic poet, if he couldn't be a madman, at least to suffer. Note as examples the works and lives of Byron, Shelley, and Coleridge. The notion was that to produce great art one had to carry a burden. Today we know that this is balderdash, but the idea had a profound influence on the eighteenth century.

Havelock Ellis, in his classic study entitled *A Study of British Genius*, found that only 44 of his 1030 geniuses, or 4.2 percent, were insane. This is proportionate to what we would expect in the population at large. One possible reason why we may link genius with madness is that geniuses are often individualistic, if not eccentric. This does not deny the fact that there have been and may be psychotic geniuses.

Not only have there been depressed artists but a number of famous scientists have been depressed. Charles Darwin, who was probably one of the four most influential individuals of the last century and a half (the other three being Marx, Freud, and Einstein), suffered from depression, among other illnesses. Intellectually, he was able to discover the theory of evolution on the basis of observing thousands of fossils. Darwin, who was the unpaid chief naturalist of the Beagle, probably wrote the most influential book of modern times, *On the Origin of Species*. He was a sickly and reclusive person for most of his adult life and his depression probably interfered with his work. Before he started his voyage of discovery he suffered from heart palpitations and chest pains and was generally miserable, gloomy, and depressed. After the voyage he couldn't cope readily with the task and put most of it away for about two years. Many tentative diagnoses have been made of his poor health, including arsenic poisoning, hysteria, and depression. No definitive conclusions can be drawn, however.

Probably the most famous statesman of the first half of the twentieth century was Sir Winston Churchill. As Prime Minister of Great Britain during England's darkest days of World War II he courageously led his nation while periodically subjected to what he called his "black dog" of depression. In fact, depression ran in Churchill's family. His ancestor the first Duke of Marlborough exhibited periods of melancholy. Benjamin Disraeli, one of Churchill's Tory predecessors as Prime Minister of Great Britain (in the 1870s), also suffered from depression. Sergei Rachmaninoff (1873–1943), pianist, composer, and conductor, had periodic bouts of depression which, at times, interfered with his creative outputs. In the United States George Washington exhibited depression-linked psychosomatic symptoms, and Abraham Lincoln's bouts of withdrawal and brooding were probably indicative of depression. In more recent times Thomas Eagleton, a temporary candidate for Vice-President, was another victim of depression.

To list the names from the creative and performing arts of those suffering in modern times from the affective disorders would provide a litany of Who's Who. These names would include William Inge, playwright, and Sylvia Plath, novelist and poet, both of whom killed themselves; Joshua Logan, playwright-producer-director, who is presently functioning effectively; and Ernest Hemingway, who had constant bouts of depression and who committed suicide. Virginia Woolf, John Berryman, Vachel Lindsay, Anne Sexton, and Hart Crane also committed suicide; and Dylan Thomas, Brendan Behan, Thomas Wolfe, and F. Scott Fitzgerald apparently drank themselves to death. The astronaut Buzz Aldrin suffered from depression but appears to have overcome it and Robert Lowell, Graham Greene, and Theodore Roethke survived their debilitating depressions. Among other things, Howard Hughes was often seriously depressed.

Many creative people from the past were attacked by the affective disorders. Sandro Botticelli (1448-1510), famous artist of the Florentine Renaissance, had deep melancholia, and Handel wrote *The Messiah*, his major oratorio, during a three-week period (August 22, 1741, to September 14, 1741), in a manic frenzy. (It is interesting to note that the advertisements for lithium, a prophylactic against the affective disorders, primarily mania, show a drawing of Handel. This raises the interesting social philosophical question whether Handel could have composed the Messiah had lithium been available to him in the eighteenth century.) Rossini, in a state of hypomania, composed the

Barber of Seville in 13 days, a prodigious feat. Robert Schumann was also a manic-depressive and his greatest moments of creativity occurred in his manic phases. When depressed he composed nothing at all.

Honoré de Balzac wrote *Cousin Bette* in six weeks. During his lifetime he produced 90 novels and stories in which he portrayed 2000 characters. Balzac, who was probably in a manic state throughout most of his life, spent money irresponsibly and was always in debt. When he wasn't busy spending money he was busy writing and would frequently stay up all night. Only a manic could write the epic work *La Comédie Humaine*. Van Gogh, the artist, in addition to being a schizophrenic was both manic and depressive.

Paradoxically, one of the most famous people to suffer from depression was Sigmund Freud. Freud's serverest problems, during the 1880s and 1890s, were *self*-diagnosed as neurasthenia (chronic mental and physical fatigue and various aches and pains) rather than melancholia. Nevertheless, the symptoms of neurasthenia and depression have much in common and it is probable that Freud was both a *neurasthenic* and a *depressive*. The important point is that at times he could not function effectively because of his ailments and occasionally (in the 1880s) tried cocaine as a means of alleviating his depressive and neurasthenic symptoms. This was restricted to the relatively brief period of his life that his biographer, Ernest Jones, calls the "Cocaine Episode."

It should be noted that not all creative people are manic-depressives nor are all manic-depressives creative. It is one thing to have the high degree of energy that exists in a manic state; it is another thing to channel it in a direction that creates new works and accomplishes effective tasks.

Approximately 22 million Americans and 2.2 million Canadians, or 10 percent of the North American population, have experienced a depressed state, and many of them never knew what hit them or when or where to seek help. It is surprising that precise statistics on the incidence of the unipolar and bipolar affective disorders do not exist. In the United States the Department of Health, Education and Welfare and in Canada the Ministry of Health keep rough estimates and in 1980 apparently 2.5 to 4.5 million North Americans had hypomanic or manic attacks. There is a thin line between those hypomanic states that enable the patient to accomplish a great deal that is useful because of the high level of manic-propelled energy and those that are harmful to the patient, family, friends, and society; for example, financial irresponsibility, felonies, promiscuity, reckless driving, and abusiveness. This is a Catch-22 situation because one of the first things "to go" during mania and hypomania is a sense of judgment. The affected person cannot judge whether his or her behavior is appropriate and if someone else says it is not the reaction may be one of hostility and abuse. In some instances a state of depression follows the manic state. Although depression is more difficult for the patient, mania is more difficult for friends and relatives to handle.

The affective disorders know no boundaries in terms of class, race, sex, religion, ethnicity, or nationality. Although I have identified some famous people who have been so stricken, I have done so primarily to indicate that a productive life can be led. People of all races and classes are affected by mood swings. Mood swings are not necessarily completely debilitating. If the diagnosis is correct, the treatment is readily available.

One of the major problems is the attitude of society toward the affective disorders and their treatment. It is not only the lay public that attaches a stigma to mental illness; it is also perpetuated by the mental health professionals themselves. Because I am a fairly well known psychologist within the Toronto mental health community, my family physician, and at one time even my psychiatrist, was concerned about protecting me lest others learn of my condition. After I had recuperated and had thought of writing this book on the chance that it might help others who were depressed, I mentioned the possibility to a psychiatrist (not the one I was seeing). He said "Norm, don't do it. You'll ruin your career. Wanting to write this book shows poor judgment on your part." I might point out that subsequently he had the courage to change his mind and has been most supportive. I should add that from the start the psychiatrist who treated me has also been most encouraging and, if I'm not mistaken, made the original suggestion that I write about my experiences.

It is to be hoped that others can benefit by my report and my presentation of some of the issues, problems, and facts with respect to the affective disorders. As a clinical psychologist who has suffered from an affective disorder, which is now under control, I believe I can provide an integration and synthesis of the experiential, clinical, and factual phenomena of the bipolar and unipolar manic-depressive disorders. By making the public aware of their nature and treatment much misery and suffering can be alleviated and the leading of more productive lives facilitated.

It is important that the climate for more research is improving. In the future it can be expected that society and the government will be more receptive and will provide the necessary research funds and that patients will be more cooperative in providing information about themselves. There should be no stigma attached to manic depression. For some persons it is part of the human condition.

3

The Dark Tunnel

On Thursday, June 2, 1977, my son and I went to see our GP. My son drove the car because I was too tense. When I entered the doctor's office I could barely speak. I was tired, irritable, anxious, sad, and unsure of myself; in short, I was depressed. After discussing my condition our family doctor said that he would arrange an appointment for me to see someone else, but in the meantime he would give me a prescription for depression (Deprex, a trade name for amitriptyline) and anxiety (diazepam, more popularly known as Valium). He insisted that I see a psychiatrist in Oshawa (30 miles east of Toronto) because I was too well known in Toronto. I suppose he was trying to protect me, but I didn't want to be protected. I saw no stigma attached to seeing a psychiatrist in Toronto. I stated that I didn't want to go to Oshawa because of the inconvenience, at which point my doctor lost his cool and threatened to put me in the hospital unless I agreed (this would be legally difficult in Ontario unless he felt that I was in imminent danger). I guess he panicked out of kindness, but I was too weak to argue with him. When I told my wife about it she immediately canceled the appointment with the psychiatrist in Oshawa.

My wife then phoned our friend Harvey, who is a psychologist at the Clarke Institute of Psychiatry (part of the Department of Psychiatry of the University of Toronto), told him that I was in bad shape, and asked his help in arranging to have me to see someone as soon as possible. After a few phone calls he called back to say that Dr. E. Persad, a psychiatrist, and Chief of the Affective Disorders Unit of the Clarke Institute of Psychiatry, would see me first thing in the morning.

Thursday afternoon, after being assured that help was near, I took my tranquilizer (diazepam) and my antidepressant (amitriptyline), which contains a sedative, and fell asleep, the first peaceful sleep I'd had in more than two months. Meanwhile, my wife, in addition to caring for me, was waiting for her parents and other members of her family to arrive in Toronto for her uncle's funeral, which was to take place Friday at noon. I don't know how my wife was able to handle this all at once, but then she is a marvelous woman. It was only recently (in December 1979) that I learned from my daughter that on that Thursday afternoon my wife told our neighbor Judy all about my plight. Judy was sympathetic and supportive and my wife finally broke down and cried. This was good for her because it allowed her to release her tensions. Beatrice, or Beatty as I call her, rarely loses her composure. In front of me, during this entire period, she showed the traditional British stiff upper lip.

That Thursday night my father-in-law and his sister arrived from Montreal and stayed at our house (my mother-in-law and sister- and brother-in-law arrived the next day). Although the house was undoubtedly noisy, I was oblivious to it all, probably as a function of my depression and the medication. I slept fairly well throughout the night, waking only once or twice. Friday morning Beatty and I headed for the Clarke Institute. We went up to the eleventh floor, gave my name to the receptionist, and at eight-thirty Dr. Persad asked me to come into his office. I thanked him for seeing me on such short notice and he asked me about my problem. I informed him that I was exhausted, tense, agitated, and anxious and mentioned my apathy, indecisiveness, and loss of appetite and sex drive. When questioned I told him that I had felt that way for about two months, and when asked what I thought prompted these feelings I said that I believed they were due primarily to the loss of my research grant and the sense of incompetence and unworthiness that followed. I was also ashamed. As Chairman of the Psychology Department at York, I had strongly emphasized the importance of research and tried to function as an exemplary model. Faculty members were encouraged to apply for research grants. Therefore I felt like a hypocrite when mine was phased out. Although I was convinced that another causal factor was the change in my relationship with Ann, for some reason I did not mention it to Dr. Persad. Perhaps I was reluctant to discuss it, although I did tell him about it a few weeks later. Of the two major factors that I believed precipitated by depression, the loss of the grant was the more significant to me. As a psychologist I naturally looked for psychological explanations and was sure that mine was a reactive depression. As it turned out it was biochemical.

Dr. Persad asked me if I had ever had these feelings before and I told him that when my father died in 1971 I had been sad and unhappy but not anxious or agitated. I had experienced grief but not a serious loss of appetite or sex drive. I did have some difficulty sleeping, but these symptoms disappeared after a few weeks. At this time (June 1977), however, I felt gripped or possessed by my symptoms and could no longer deal with day-to-day tasks.

We discussed my childhood and youth and I couldn't recall anything specifically significant other than that I had ranked second in elementary school and was disappointed that I wasn't first in my high-school class. I had never really felt like a winner until after I had my doctorate, but then I had never really felt like a loser. There were four of us in our immediate family: my father, who was a cutter in men's clothing, my mother, and my older sister, a social worker who is now married to a political scientist, and myself. Although our family was not religious, we were traditional and observed all the Jewish holidays. I was married when I was 24 and my wife 20, and we had two children. We had a good marriage. And now I was agitated and bewildered.

During the interview with Dr. Persad I was in a fog. The thing I remembered most clearly, however, is that he treated me with sympathy, dignity, and respect—as if I counted, as if I were important, even though I didn't feel important. I was pleased that he called me doctor. Physicians often refer only to themselves as doctor and call everyone else Mr., even though the Ph.D. degree is an older and more venerable degree than the M.D. We psychologists are particularly sensitive (some would even say paranoid) on this point. Perhaps it is because psychiatrists have a securer position and higher status in society than psychologists. In any case, I felt that I was being treated as an equal by Dr. Persad rather than in a one-down position. This boosted my self-esteem and self-respect. Although I was depressed, I usually felt better with Dr. Persad or shortly after seeing him. Nevertheless, I also had a morbid and unrealistic fear that he was going to hospitalize me.

Dr. Persad then called Beatty in and recommended that I gradually increase the dosage of the antidepressant drug and continue with the tranquilizers. He took blood tests to check my thyroid level because a malfunctioning thyroid can produce some of the symptoms of depression. He told me to come again the following Wednesday, June 8, but to be sure to phone if there were any major reactions before then. I believe that he also told Beatty not to leave me home alone. (My guess is that he was concerned about the possibility of suicide, which is always a potential risk with depressed persons. I might point out, however, that throughout my illness I never had any suicidal thoughts. I probably felt too incompetent to attempt or even contemplate suicide).

Throughout my treatment Dr. Persad always made certain that I was present whenever he asked to speak to Beatty. He never went behind my back and I trusted him completely. Trust between a therapist and patient is one of the basic ingredients of an effective therapeutic relationship. It is also a two-way street. The patient must trust and have faith in the therapist. The patient must follow the instructions of the therapist, especially with respect to medication, and the therapist must trust the patient to follow them.

One of my major problems was the difficulty I had in accepting the fact of my illness. Another is that I hate to take pills and rarely need as much as an aspirin. Therefore my attitude toward the medication prescribed was anything but positive, but I did agree to take the antidepressants and tranquilizers, although reluctantly. Dr. Persad told me that it would be about three weeks before any major changes could be produced and that as the dosage was increased there might be side effects, many of which I developed, such as dryness of the mouth, constipation, drowsiness, and possibly urinary retention. What didn't help is that I had a copy of the *Compendium of Pharmaceuticals and Specialities* (CPS), published by the Canadian Pharmaceutical Association, a book that lists the various drugs, their indications, contraindications, precautions, adverse effects, and dosages. My problem was that I knew too much for my own good—too much about depression and too much about medication. I also had too many of the psychologist's biases against psychiatry. My sophistication was a two-edged sword. On the one hand, I was easier to treat because I could understand what was happening; on the other hand, treating me was more difficult because I couldn't really accept the fact that I was sick.

I knew about the side effects of the medication, I knew that antidepressants took three weeks to produce major changes, and I knew that I hated taking them. This did not make the task any easier. I knew that there were two major classes of antidepressant drugs, namely, the tricyclics and the monoamine oxidase (MAO) inhibitors. Both drugs increase the amount of noradrenaline (a chemical in the nervous system) between nerve fibers, but do so in two ways. (The more technically minded reader is referred to Chapter 6, which presents a detailed account of these drugs, how they were discovered, and the biochemical and physiological bases on which they operate.) It is believed that a major cause of depression is a deficiency of noradrenaline between nerve fibers. An enzyme called monoamine oxidase arrests its production; the MAO inhibitor (e.g., Parnate) antidepressant drugs nullify the effects of monoamine oxidase and therefore increases the supply of noradrenaline between nerve fibers. The tricyclic drugs (amitriptyline drugs like Levate or Elavil) operate directly on the transmission of noradrenaline by increasing the amount between nerve fibers. For the most part the tricyclic drugs are preferred to the MAO inhibitors for treating depression. The MAO inhibitors can have potentially dangerous side effects and usually require dietary restrictions (e.g., aged cheese, pickled herring, beer, wine, and chocolate are to be avoided) for those individuals who take the pills. Therefore I perceived my tricyclic prescription (amitriptyline) as the lesser of two evils. I agreed to continue taking the antidepressants and tranquilizers, as Dr. Persad suggested, but I was not enthusiastic about the idea.

Lost Weekend

We returned home about 10 o'clock and Beatty had to get ready for her uncle's funeral at noon. A number of people were staying at our house, but for all practical purposes I was aware of none of them. Judy was going to "babysit" with me part of the time while everyone was at the funeral and Ann was coming over for the rest. Ann arrived shortly before the funeral but announced that she had to dash off to see a friend and would come back later. With Judy present to "mind" me, I took my medication and went to bed. Ann must have returned within the hour because I heard her talking to Judy in the kitchen. They both stayed until my daughter returned from school.

During most of the afternoon I slept or lay in a daze. In fact, I was in a dazed state most of that weekend. I vaguely remember visitors and relatives coming and going, but I was too exhausted and too depressed to see them. By Tuesday or Wednesday I felt slightly better but not enough to function properly or to go to work. Beatty had called my office the day I went to see the doctor and told my administrative assistant and secretary that I was sick and would not be coming to the office. She also asked that arrangements be made for a colleague to read my papers at the Canadian Psychological Association meetings in Vancouver. I discovered later that both my secretary and administrative assistant were very upset because I was ill. They were then and still are very fond of me.

One of the things I was worried about concerned a substitute to run the department while I was absent. I had been at York since 1960 and had never missed a day's work because of illness. Although classes were over and there wasn't much administrative work to do, there are always odds and ends to attend to in the chairman's office; for example, last minute changes in teaching assignments, hiring of part-time instructors and teaching assistants, and authorizing money for faculty members' expenses at conferences and meetings. As chairman I tended to focus on crises and let my administrative assistant and secretary handle the day-to-day details of the department. I had discovered early in my chairmanship that many of the crises were not really mine but those of other people who hoped that I would solve them. Usually I applied my 48-to-72-hour waiting rule; that is, when very important problems had to be resolved I usually waited two or three days before making a decision. Much to my pleasant surprise most of them disappeared by then. There is altogether too much time spent on administrative trivia, especially at universities. Perhaps the reason is that the stakes are so small.

It was obvious to me, at this point, that I could not function effectively as chairman, at least for the next few weeks. Therefore I asked Morris to cover for me and to consult with another member of the Executive Committee in case there were any emergencies that he, Morris, could not handle. Morris agreed and I was comforted.

One week later (about June 10) I found out that the member of the Executive Committee had taken over as Acting Chairman of the Department. He and Morris had gone to see the Dean and had informed him that they would be covering for me, jointly. Subsequently, the committee member informed Morris that he could handle things by himself and Morris agreed. He then sent out a memo to the Department in which he stated that I was suffering from exhaustion, that he didn't know when I would be back, and that he was in charge. I felt psychologically undressed.

My research assistant told me about the memo but I was too depressed, anxious, and upset to do anything about it. (I did not actually see the memo until September.) My administrative assistant bought a big get well card, which everyone signed, and the new acting chairman brought it to me. Every few weeks he would visit me at home and fill me in on what was happening—more than I cared to know. (He tried hard and made a point of keeping me informed.)

I returned to see Dr. Persad on Wednesday, June 8. Although I felt a little better, I was still upset at being incapacitated. I guess I really couldn't accept the fact that I was sick. Dr. Persad asked me to increase the dosage of the antidepressant (Levate, another trade name for amitriptyline, the most common being Elavil) from 75 to 100 mg and to see him again in a week. By Friday, June 10, however, I had become more agitated and bewildered and I developed a morbid fear of being hospitalized. Beatty phoned Dr. Persad, who kindly arranged an appointment. Seeing Dr. Persad had a calming effect on me, but I was still depressed. I was becoming extremely indecisive and very tired and everything became an effort for me. One of the hardest things was getting up in the morning. Although I had had some sleep, I felt as if a ton of bricks was resting on me. It had become extremely difficult to get out of bed. I was lethargic and drowsy, probably because of the depression and heavy medication.

My indecisiveness was the worst of all. I couldn't decide what to eat or what to wear. I couldn't decide whether to get out of bed or to stay. I couldn't decide whether to shower or not to shower. I could never decide what I wanted to do because I didn't know myself. I was completely apathetic. My wife showed great patience and tolerance throughout all this. I don't know how she maintained her composure. If I had had to deal with someone as indecisive as I was, I'd have been driven around the bend. Time seemed to move so very slowly for me. I couldn't read, I couldn't play tennis, I couldn't drive my car, and I couldn't work. After much persuasion on Beatty's part I occasionally went for a walk. In general, I lived in a fog of bewilderment. I was unhappy, confused, lacking in self-confidence and self-esteem, and sure that I was going to be hospitalized. This really scared me.

I saw Dr. Persad again on Wednesday, June 15, at which time he increased the dosage of the antidepressant to 150 mg, which is a minimal effective therapeutic dose, but I had to see him again on Friday, June 17, because of my greatly increased agitation. First I was anxious about being hospitalized, although this had no basis in fact. Second, I was convinced that I had not worked effectively as a consultant at the Toronto East General, that I was a fraud, and that the Department of Psychiatry at the Hospital was disappointed in my performance, all of which had no basis in fact. Beatty phoned Tom Schofield, who was Chief of Psychiatry at the Toronto East General Hospital at that time and a close friend of ours, and Tom came over to see us Saturday morning on the way to his summer cottage. He reassured me that he was extremely pleased with my performance and only hoped that I would get better quickly. Tom was a constant source of comfort to Beatty and me during my illness.

The next day, Sunday, I was once again extremely depressed and started to cry. This time my guilt concerned my relationship with Ann, and what I considered my disloyalty to Beatty. I told Beatty why I was upset and that I regretted my emotional involvement with Ann. Beatty was very comforting. She had known all along that I had become infatuated with Ann (wives always know!), and although she (Beatty) was hurt she was not extremely upset because she realized that I would get over it. Beatty perceived this infatuation as a temporary aberration related to the excitement of running around, doing different things, and playing too much tennis. Although Beatty was reassuring, I was still unhappy.

During this time the antidepressant was beginning to work. During this time, also, I developed one of the side effects of the antidepressant drug—namely, difficulty in urinating—which became worse and I more and more anxious. In fact, the very anticipation of urinating made me anxious. My whole life revolved around whether I would be able to urinate. It was taking me longer and longer each time. In fact, sometimes I could urinate only while sitting down. I had a horror of being sent to the emergency ward of a general hospital to have my bladder pumped. One morning (it was always worse in the morning) I couldn't urinate at all. I became hysterical and insisted that Beatty phone Dr. Persad immediately. He recommended that I take a tranquilizer and go off the antidepressant. By noon I was able to urinate and within the next day or so I had no further trouble. But my depression got worse, especially on waking in the early morning. By this time Dr. Persad had diagnosed my illness as a unipolar depression.

About a week after I went off the antidepressants we went out to dinner with some friends and I really felt alert. I got dressed up for the evening and enjoyed myself thoroughly. During the entire night I planned what I would be doing when I returned to work. Although I couldn't sleep all night, I wasn't worried. I rested in bed until breakfast time and then got up without any difficulty. After breakfast I put on a jacket and tie (I rarely wear a tie) in preparation for my appointment with Dr. Persad. I also phoned my office and told my secretary and administrative assistant I would be in to work in a few days. The only medication I was taking was the tranquilizers—about 15 to 20 mg a day of diazepam. I was on top of the world. After seeing Dr. Persad Beatty and I went to lunch and then home. Beatty came with me to the Clarke Institute for every appointment because I still wasn't driving. Furthermore, I may have reasoned that by having Beatty with me I would be protected from being hospitalized. I usually saw Dr. Persad alone.

On returning home I prepared a memorandum for the Department of Psychology at York University, in which I pointed out that the news of my demise had been greatly exaggerated, that I was recuperating, and that I would be returning to work shortly. Fortunately, Irwin, a colleague who was visiting me, persuaded me not to send it. No doubt I was behaving in a hypomanic fashion and my judgment was not so good as it might have been. As it turned out, I didn't go back to work that next week or even that month.

About midafternoon I began to feel tense, irritable, and jumpy. I rested for about two hours and then had dinner. Later we were to have guests for coffee and dessert. Beatty's aunt (whose husband had died at the beginning of June) and her aunt's sister and brother-in-law were coming over. By nine-thirty, when no one had arrived, I was getting jumpier and jumpier, agitated, and anxious. I had a lump in my throat and also felt rejected. At about ten o'clock Beatty's relatives arrived— they had been lost, which was reasonable because they had moved to Toronto only at the beginning of May. We then sat down to have dessert. By that time I was so much on edge I could barely sit still. I felt awful and too agitated to interact. I excused myself—the first and only time I have ever done so in my life—and went to lie down on my bed. I couldn't lie still. Beatty finally undressed me and I fell into a deep sleep, throughly exhausted. The next morning June 25, 1977, I woke up feeling drained, tired, and in a fog.

4

The Season in Darkness

Saturday, June 25, 1977, was the day before my twenty-second wedding anniversary. It was also the most depressing day of my life. I literally could not raise myself out of bed. About 10 o'clock, when I awoke, the first thing I remember saying to Beatty was "This is qualitatively different. I feel as if I were carrying a ton of bricks." I was completely exhausted, physically and mentally, and emotionally drained. Actually, I was too tired to be in a state of panic, but I didn't really know what to do. After about an hour my wife phoned the Clarke Institute and tried to reach Dr. Persad. Since it was Saturday, he was not on duty. Beatty left a message for him to return her call and also asked the telephone receptionist what should be done. She was told to bring me down to the out-patient department if my condition didn't improve. Knowing my concern about being hospitalized, she was reluctant to comply.

During this time I stayed in bed, too exhausted to do anything else. By noon there had been no noticeable change in my condition. Beatty then phoned Harvey, who had referred us to Dr. Persad, and asked him for advice. Harvey told Beatty to call the duty doctor at the Clarke and added that if we couldn't reach Dr. Persad, and my condition stabilized, the most sensible thing would be to keep me at home.

Shortly after noon one of my colleagues phoned to say she wanted to see me, but I was not up to seeing anyone and we asked her to come at another time. I must point out that this was the only time during my entire illness that I was unable to receive visitors. The one thing I did enjoy was talking to my friends. Many of them came and I found their calls quite therapeutic. People were genuinely concerned. I especially remember how worried my friend and accountant Donald was when he learned that I was ill. Being with other people made me feel human

again. I usually thrive in social situations and have the "gift of gab."
This time, however, I wanted to be left alone.

By three o'clock I began to feel better and was able to move about in
bed and by four I could sit up. Kathy, another colleague, phoned to ask
if she could visit me. Beatty was about to tell her that it would not be
appropriate when I shouted "yes, I would like her to come." Perhaps
what helped was that she was our very close friend. Kathy came over
later in the evening and I got up to receive her. I was still depressed but I
had recovered from the extreme fatigue. I didn't know what had hit me.

Later on I discovered that my "collapse" was in response to the
sudden cessation of the antidepressant drug. The prime reaction was the
hypomanic behavior which led to exhaustion, fatigue, and withdrawal.
This attests to the importance of withdrawing from a drug gradually
rather than going off it "cold turkey." My reaction was biochemical
and physiological. I had had withdrawal symptoms.

The next day, June 26, was our twenty-second wedding anniversary,
normally a joyous occasion. Beatty and I went to a friend's house for
lunch and although I still felt listless and indecisive I joined in the
conversation. It was a warm, sunny day, and it was great to get outside
after lying in bed most of the day before. Relatively speaking it was a
good day. However, I was frustrated by the fact that here it was my
anniversary, a time to be happy and gay, but instead I was dejected and
apathetic. What a contrast! On Monday Beatty phoned Dr. Persad and
told him what had happened on Saturday and he arranged to see me on
Wednesday. Because he hadn't received our last message he gave us his
unlisted home number and told us to phone him there in an emergency.

On Wednesday Dr. Persad prescribed imipramine (trade name
Tofranil), which is a different form of antidepressant. On June 18, when
I first experienced urinary retention, he had prescribed Sinequan, which
is also different from amitriptyline. This, too, had been discontinued. I
believe that he started me off on 75 mg of Tofranil and told me to
increase the dosage gradually. I was certain that I was going to have
more urinary problems with this drug and I did. On the way home from
Dr. Persad's office, even before we had the prescription filled I
expressed the fear that I would have difficulty urinating after taking
Tofranil. I was really worried about it. (Chapter 6 presents a technical
discussion of antidepressant drugs.)

That night I took the Tofranil before I went to bed, and sure enough I had a bit of trouble urinating the next morning, but nothing like the extreme difficulty and resulting hysteria I had had 10 days earlier in reaction to the amitriptyline. I took Valium with the Tofranil to help me relax, but in many ways it was the anticipation of urinating rather than the actual act that provoked the anxiety.

Thursday night my wife and I went out for dinner and then for a walk. I was slightly more relaxed. The next day, July 1, was Canada Day, a federal holiday. I borrowed my son's bicycle and rode it for a few blocks. This produced a great sense of accomplishment because I had done nothing worthwhile since the beginning of June. Besides, the exercise was good for me. My son recognized my need for positive action, to do something that would give me a lift. I felt supported and encouraged.

Friday afternoon the Dean of Arts phoned and asked to see me before he left on vacation. I was delighted that he wanted to visit me but suspicious of his motive for coming to see me at home. Could it be to assess my competence to continue as chairman? My wife insisted that the Dean was genuinely interested in my welfare and was coming to see me because I was ill. The Dean was most sympathetic, compassionate, and understanding. He told me not to worry, that "my zoo" (the department) hadn't erupted, and that I was probably doing no less than the chairmen who were in good health. (This was the summer and nothing much was going on anyhow.) The Dean was actually very fond of me and believed that I had done an excellent job as chairman of the Psychology Department.

On Saturday Harvey took me to see the Blue Jays play baseball. I followed the game for about two or three innings but became preoccupied with having to urinate. I was afraid to go to the men's room for two reasons. First, I was concerned that I might have difficulty urinating and be embarrassed in the public washroom. Second, I thought I might not be able to find my way back to my seat. I was beginning to develop a fear of getting lost. Harvey took me home, where I found Graham, the Dean of Graduate Studies, who is a psychologist and my friend, waiting for me. He had been away in France when I became ill and had not seen me since that time. I excused myself and after 10 or 15 minutes was able to urinate.

I was pleased to see Graham because, among other things, he is perceptive, utterly charming, and extremely witty. After I told him about my symptoms he said that it was quite clear to him that my depression was not a reactive one, that it was undoubtedly biochemical (endogenous or unipolar), and that as soon as the depression lifted I would be back to normal almost at once. I looked him square in the eye and said "Graham, you are full of shit." As it turned out he was 100 percent correct and I was wrong (Dr. Persad had also diagnosed my illness as a unipolar affective disorder). Even though I disagreed with Graham's diagnosis (I still believed my depression was reactive) I was delighted to see him and it cheered me up to be with him (a few weeks later when I saw him again I assumed incorrectly that he really wanted to determine whether I was competent).

The next day Morris came to visit me. I was having extreme difficulty urinating and by noon was again in a state of hysteria. Beatty and Morris persuaded me to phone Dr. Persad at home. I was reluctant to do so because I didn't want to distrub him. I did phone him, however, and was told to stop taking the Tofranil and to see him on Tuesday. He also told me not to take any more antidepressants but to continue with the Valium.

When I saw him July 14 he found me bewildered and agitated and decided that I needed a stronger tranquilizer than diazepam (Valium). He therefore prescribed Thioril, which is a form of phenothiazine and equivalent to Mellaril. He prescribed nothing further because of my negative reaction to antidepressants. He told me to take only the tranquilizer and to return in about 10 days. (On June 3 I had started with amitriptyline, which is Levate or Elavil. On June 18 I switched to Sinequan, and on June 29 to Tofranil or imipramine. On July 3 I discontinued all antidepressants.)

While taking the Thioril I became calmer but still lacked self-confidence and was moderately depressed. I did drive our car once or twice for the first time since the beginning of June (but not until at least six hours after taking Thioril because like all tranquilizers it has a drowsy effect). The Thioril did calm me down and diminish my agitation, but in some ways I was like a zombie. I felt as if I were living in an opaque envelope. I recall going sailing on Lake Ontario with some friends, and even though the boat almost tipped I felt no anxiety. It was as if I were protected by a shell or cocoon. It was the hottest day of the year, about 98 degrees Fahrenheit, but I was oblivious to the heat. That night we went to a football game. I felt as if I were floating on air. My only concern was the glucose tolerance test I had to take the next day. This meant that I could drink nothing but water after nine o'clock. About five minutes to nine I drank about a quart of cola, which was not too wise. As it turned out the results of the test were negative and my worries were all for nothing.

About the third week in July Dr. Persad told me that he would be going away for about three weeks in August. He would, however, arrange to have me see a regular staff psychiatrist at the Clarke, who was also a consultant in the Affective Disroders Unit. Dr. Persad knew that I was worried and upset about his being away but persuaded me that everything was going to be fine and arranged for a consultation with Dr. Stancer the following week. For some reason I failed to tell Dr. Persad about my sensation of being enveloped after taking the Thioril.

Dr. Stancer took my case history and we discussed various alternative courses of treatment. He confirmed the diagnosis of depression and said that because I had had so much trouble with the tricyclic antidepressants (amitriptyline and imipramine) another possibility was the use of mono amine oxidase (MAO) inhibitors, which, as indicated in Chapter 3, were a different class of antidepressants from the tricyclic groups of drugs. Because of their biochemical reactions, MAO inhibitors precluded all food that contains tyramine. The prohibited items were cheese (especially processed cheeses), bananas, alcohol, liver, Bovril, cream, pickled herring, yogurt, wine (especially red wine), excessive caffeine, chocolate, and, in general, anything fermented, all of which in conjunction with the MAO inhibitors, could lead to hypertension. This would be especially difficult for me because I'm a chocolate freak and also like cheese of-all kinds. (Persons on the MAO inhibitors are also prohibited from taking tricyclic antidepressants, antidiabetics, amphetamines, anesthetics, Inderal, which is prescribed for heart disease, and various cough medicines. Aspirin, codeine, and antibiotics are permitted. We discussed the MAO inhibitors and how they work in Chapter 3.) Chapter 6 presents a more detailed and technical discussion of these drugs. The MAO inhibitor that Dr. Stancer suggested was Parnate.

An alternative course of treatment (to the Parnate) was electroshock or electroconvulsive therapy, commonly known as ECT. I was aghast. For reasons given in Chapter 7 I had strong negative reactions even to the thought of ECT and refused to discuss it as a course of treatment.

Dr. Stancer pointed out that ECT was the safest form of combatting depression and that after 6 to 12 sessions a person could function effectively. He told me about a surgeon who went back to work in the operating room the day after his last ECT treatment. Nevertheless, for the present we agreed on Parnate. I was to start with two tablets of 10 mg each (20 mg per day) for a few days and then increased the dosage to 30 mg and 50 mg. It was important to take all the medication before 2 P.M. to avoid lying awake all night. I readily agreed to the treatment, more in desperation and fear of being hospitalized than in any belief that the treatment would be helpful. I was to see Dr. Persad once more before he went on vacation and Dr. Stancer informed me that he too would be away for a few days the following week. Although a staff member would be covering, this did not boost my self-confidence.

One of my major difficulties was the conviction that at times I was being treated as a colleague rather than a patient. This created a problem for me and for the psychiatrists. Because I was, in effect, a colleague, their manner toward me was not condescending (this is not meant to imply that they treat others condescendingly), and I think that they were uncomfortable in the doctor-patient relationship. On the other hand, I was ill and a patient and needed to be cared for like a patient. I myself had ambivalent feelings in this regard. Dr. Stancer, at one point, admitted that it was difficult to treat colleagues as patients. At times it placed both my doctors and me in a difficult position. If anything, they were too kind to me. Both Dr. Persad and Dr. Stancer are compassionate men and were distressed because I was taking so long to get well. I guess this is one of the dilemmas to be faced when one professional must prescribe for another.

After seeing Dr. Stancer and before filling the prescription for Parnate, my wife, my two children, and I went out to dinner at a nice French restaurant called La Bodega. I wanted one last fling before starting on the Parnate and the restrictive diet that it involved. The meal was enjoyable, but I was becoming worried about the possible side effects of the drug and about the fact that I was not getting any better after two months of treatment for my depression. Later that evening Morris and his future wife brought me some delicious pastries, including chocolate eclairs, which I devoured voraciously, knowing that this would be my last chance to enjoy chocolate for some time.

On Thursday, August 4, I started on the Parnate. The strategy was to start with two tablets of 10 mg each, one in the morning and one at noon, three tablets a few days later, and then five tablets, or 50 mg, after about five days. It was essential, however, that all the medication be taken before two o'clock in the afternoon. Otherwise I would have trouble falling asleep at night. The Parnate had an activating effect.

Except for my anxiety about eating the wrong things, the next few days were uneventful. Ann asked if she could give Beatty some respite by taking me out to lunch on Tuesday. It was getting tiresome for Beatty to have to look after me all the time. At times I acted like a child. Perhaps I needed a babysitter! In the morning I went to the barber shop by myself for a haircut. I then returned home and took the rest of my Parnate. This was the first day that I increased the dosage to 50 mg. Ann picked me up and we went out to lunch at a neighborhood delicatessen.

I had a pastrami sandwich and tea, neither of which was on my prohibited list. After lunch we went over to Baskin-Robbins for an ice cream cone. In general, I think I was rather poor company and was pretty much out of it. I was too preoccupied with myself. Ann then drove me back home and left me in the driveway.

No one was home. As I walked into the living room a sudden terrible pounding in my head was accompanied by acute nausea. I went into the bedroom and lay down on the bed. I broke into a cold sweat. After about 20 minutes Beatty returned from shopping and I told her how I felt. The pounding got worse and the chills ran up and down my spine. I asked Beatty to take me over to the emergency ward at the North York General Hospital, for I suspected correctly that I was experiencing a high blood pressure (hypertension) reaction to the Parnate.

At North York General my blood pressure was 220 systolic (maximum pressure in blood vessels when the heart beats or contracts) over 110 diastolic (minimum pressure in blood vessels when the heart relaxes between beats or contractions). This was dangerously high. The intern on duty (who was new) told me that I was suffering from hypertension. I explained to him that I was having a reaction to Parnate and he went to look it up in the CPS. He obviously didn't know what Parnate was. While he was gone I vomited and then felt slightly better. My blood pressure dropped to 180 over 100 and he told me to go home and rest. Obviously he should have kept me at the hospital under observation until my blood pressure dropped to normal. When we got home Beatty called Dr. M. at the Clarke, who was covering for Dr. Stancer. Dr. M.

was astonished to learn that I had been discharged from the hospital with such a high blood pressure reading. He pointed out that the Clarke had no facilities for monitoring blood pressure but that he would call our general practitioner and arrange to have me readmitted to North York General (Dr. M. did not have admitting privileges at the North York General and therefore it was necessary to get the help of our GP). A few minutes later our doctor phoned us at home and told Beatty to take me back to emergency at the North York General. He said I could go right in. When I got there, however, I had to go through the usual red tape and fill out the usual forms.

This time the duty doctor was an internist who knew what he was doing. My blood pressure was then 160/100. I was told that I would have to stay overnight for observation and was placed in a room adjacent to the emergency department. I informed the nurses that I was on Parnate and a restricted diet. The doctor had ordered a soft diet (which was not necessarily free of chocolate or cheese). Obviously, the nurses were clueless about Parnate. When I refused to eat everything on my plate they called me uncooperative, but they did give me my tranquilizer. I believe at that time I was back on Valium. Throughout the night they monitored my blood pressure, waking me every hour to take it. Because it had dropped to 120/70, I was released the next morning (Wednesday). Dr. M. had told me not to take Parnate that day but to start again on Thursday.

Even though I was extremely tired (I had been up half the night having my blood pressure taken), Beatty, Harvey, and I went to the Stratford Shakespeare Festival as planned. We had a picnic lunch, but I was afraid to eat lest my blood pressure rise again. The play was supposed to be good, but in my groggy state I had no way of knowing. I could barely keep my eyes open. But it was nice being out of the hospital. After the play we drove back to Toronto in the rain and decided to have dinner at the Richelieu. I was hesitant about going to the Richelieu for two reasons. First, the Dean of Arts sometimes dined at that particular restaurant and I didn't want him to see me there: I felt guilty about going out to dinner when I was not going to the office. What if the Dean thought I was malingering? My second reason for concern was that some of the food in this French restaurant would trigger another attack of hypertension. I was really becoming paranoid about what I ate. There was no serious cause for concern.

The next day, Thursday, I took two tablets of of Parnate in the morning and three at noon. I had a tuna fish sandwich (which does not contain tyramine and therefore was not on the prohibited food list) for lunch. About a half-hour after lunch and the noontime Parnate my head began to pound. Wow, what a headache! My wife phoned our GP, who was out for the moment. Instead we went over to see his associate and explained what had happened. My blood pressure was 180/110. The doctor told me to lie down and rest in his office. After a half-hour he took my blood pressure again. It was 160/110. He then arranged to have me admitted at the North York General, where once again I had to explain that my high blood pressure was a reaction to Parnate. I spent the night at the hospital and was discharged the next day by my GP. My blood pressure was down to 120/70. Beatty had phoned Dr. M. at the Clarke and I was told not to take any more Parnate. Evidently, I was reacting to the drug itself and not to anything I had eaten. Perhaps I was allergic to Parnate or perhaps there was something in the tuna fish that was incompatible with it. In any case, I was worn out by my bouts with this particular medication.

Because it takes a week or two for the MAO inhibitor to be cleared out of one's system, I was overly cautious about what I ate, for I feared another attack of hypertension. In fact, I was downright paranoid about it. I questioned my wife about everything she served to make certain that there was nothing (e.g., fermented foods, processed cheese, liver, or wine) to which I might be allergic. Beatty was patient, tolerant, and understanding thought it all. No doubt I was pretty obnoxious, but nobody had the heart to tell me because I was so deeply depressed. On Saturday one of my colleagues from the Toronto East General Hospital, Department of Psychiatry, and a former student of mine, came over for lunch. We had a nice visit and I was pleased to see her. However, I was very picky during lunch and left half of it on my plate. She was kind enough not to comment on my behavior, for I was really worried that I would have a bad hypertensive reaction.

The following Tuesday (August 16) I called on Dr. Stancer again. I was so disturbed that I was shaking like a leaf before I entered his office. Because the Parnate was not working I was positive that he was going to "flip me" into the hospital, as I put it. Beatty told me not to be silly. Dr. Stancer said that he was extremely sorry that I had had so much trouble with Parnate and was also sorry that he was out of town

when all this happened. He wasn't really certain what to suggest next
and was concerned because the depression was lasting so long. He
finally prescribed Aventyl, another of the tricyclic antidepressant drugs,
which is the chemical nortriptyline, unlike Levate, Deprex, and Elavil,
which are defined chemically as amitriptyline. (Both amitriptyline and
nortriptyline are dibenzocyloheptines. The chemical breakdown and
absorption of the two in the body are slightly different.) Dr. Stancer
prescribed four capsules of 25 mg each, or 100 mg a day. I was to start
on Wednesday, August 17, 1977.

I did not sleep well on the night of Tuesday, August 16. What
troubled me was that I had been off Parnate for only a week and here I
was told to start again on the tricyclic antidepressants. The first thing I
did when I awoke on Wednesday morning was to look up Aventyl in
my CPS. Sure enough, under Aventyl it said, among other things,
"Should not be given concomitantly with or within at least 14 days
following the discontinuance of a MAO inhibitor." What were they
trying to do with me? I had Beatty phone Dr. Stancer because I was too
nervous to talk. He was busy and his secretary said he would phone
back when he was free. I spent the whole morning pacing the hall like a
wounded lion in his cage. I was so agitated that my pacing almost wore
a hole in the rug.

Dr. Stancer phoned back at about noon and asked Beatty to put me
on the phone. He really blasted me. He accused me of wanting to be my
own doctor and to prescribe my own medicine and my own course of
treatment, which is, of course, an impossible task. He said he knew
what he was doing (he certainly did because, in addition to his M.D., he
had a Ph.D. in biochemistry), that the CPS errs on the side of caution,
and that it was certainly safe to take the Aventyl. Intellectually, I
believed him. I'm not certain that I did emotionally.

My wife and son stood over me and made sure that I took my
medication. I took the Aventyl with reluctance. As I said, intellectually
I knew there would be no harm in my taking this medication;
emotionally I was still quite apprehensive. By this time I was also
getting discouraged with my progress because I wasn't getting any
better. Here it was mid-August and I hadn't shown much improvement
since my collapse at the beginning of June. Ten weeks is a long time to
be out of it. After a few days I started having some difficulty urinating
but psyched myself out of it by saying to myself that Dr. Stancer would

be angry with me if I didn't. Although it sometimes took me 15 to 20 minutes, I was able to urinate without becoming hysterical. What was more upsetting was my paranoia about what I was eating. At times I was fairly close to developing a food phobia and was certain that I would be getting an adverse reaction to any food as a result of having taken Parnate in the past.

During all this time my family showed great tolerance and patience. This was all the more remarkable because my daughter, aged 15 (almost 16), had to go to the hospital to have four impacted wisdom teeth removed. She was brave and mature about her ordeal. I was cowardly and immature about mine. Depression can do strange things to a person. After a while everything began to seem hopeless. As a result of my long illness, I was developing a secondary depression.

During the week of August 15–22 the Rothmans Canadian Tennis was held at the York Tennis Centre. Even though I had a ticket for the series, I was reluctant to go. Beatty and my friends finally persuaded me to go on Monday night, August 15. My wife drove me over to a friend's house and I was to get a ride with Kathy, who was having dinner there. My feelings about going were ambivalent. I do love tennis, but I was afraid I wouldn't be able to cope with the crowds or that I might get lost, and I was also ashamed to have people see the bad shape that I was still in. When my wife drove me up to the house I asked her to stay until I went inside. Even though there were three cars in the driveway, I was sure that I had been deserted and that everyone had left in a fourth. I was really becoming mistrustful and suspicious. Beatty humored me and waited until I waved to show her that everything was OK. I must have looked silly but no one said anything. In fact, everyone was pleased to see me and delighted that I was able to go with them.

Kathy and I sat for a while in two box seats that belonged to York University, but when we started back to our regular seats I was positive that I was going to get lost. Kathy may have been aware of this, for she made certain not to walk too quickly to alleviate my anxiety. She didn't really think that I would get lost but I certainly thought I did. I was beginning to feel disoriented and was looking for familiar faces to help me to find my seat. All of us probably do this most of the time, but we react so automatially that we don't really think about it. Being depressed, I was positive that I was becoming disoriented and that I would be deserted. Despite all this, I enjoyed the tennis and was pleased to be outdoors. In fact, I went almost every day and on the days that I didn't go I gave my ticket to my son.

On Thursday, when my wife took our daughter to the hospital to have her wisdom teeth extracted, Beatty insisted that I go to York University and the tennis matches. My son drove me to my office at the university and I must admit that I was tense about being there, but I did manage to talk to my secretary, administrative assistant, and some of my colleagues without apparent difficulty. I was extremely worried about finding my way from the Psychology Building to the Tennis Centre. My son walked me over to the front gates, but because he didn't have a ticket he was not permitted to enter. With great trepidation I passed through the side door of the Tennis Centre and headed in the general direction of my seat. What a great relief to look down and see Kathy. Another major accomplishment. I had found my way to my seat all by myself.

After an hour or so I'd had enough, so I found my way back to the Psychology Building and my son drove me home. Just as we arrived Beatty returned from the hospital with our daughter. I was pleased to see everyone. My wife informed me that all had gone well, but that our daughter's face would probably swell and that she would be in pain for a week or so. There was also the possibility of bleeding. By that evening she looked like a chipmunk, but she was very brave about the whole matter. I was terribly worried that something might happen to her.

Friday was fairly uneventful, but on Friday night my daughter's gums started bleeding. My wife phoned the dentist, who suggested that tea bags be placed on my daughter's gums, where the molars had been, since the tannin in the tea would cause clotting and stop the bleeding. My wife handled this in a cool and efficient manner and it worked. I was upset and anxious and started pacing up and down the hall. I was afraid something was going to happen to my daughter. Of course nothing did. She herself behaved in a very mature manner.

On Tuesday when I went to see Dr. Stancer I was again afraid that he might hospitalize me. The Aventyl hadn't had any effect, but of course, it was still too early because it usually takes about three weeks until the tricyclic antidepressants are effective. By this time I had become impatient and discouraged. I had the feeling that Dr. Stancer himself wasn't certain what to do next. He was probably reluctant at this point to raise the question of ECT because he knew how I felt about it.

On Saturday morning Kurt, a colleague and close friend of mine, phoned me to ask if I wanted to go for a walk. Kurt was most supportive and helpful to me throughout my illness. I said I would be pleased to go but then was in a conflict because I also wanted to see the tennis that afternoon. Nevertheless, late in the morning we went for a walk in the woods outside Toronto. It was a beautiful day and I was soothed and relaxed. However, after about a half hour I became jittery and jumpy because I didn't want to miss the tennis matches. Kurt was very understanding. When we got home Beatty invited him to lunch with us, and I felt guilty about wanting to go to the tennis matches and being delayed because of lunch. Furthermore, I was still worried about my food. Nevertheless, after lunch Kurt let me off at the parking lot at York. I made it to the tennis courts and to my seat by myself.

During all this time I was physically exhausted. I still hadn't caught up on the sleep I had lost the two nights that I was hospitalized by my reaction to Parnate and had been awakened every hour to have my blood pressure checked. I was also exhausted by my depression. Even though I had been up for two nights, I was unable to sleep during the day. The day after the first Parnate incident we went to Stratford and the day after the second I stayed up all day.

By this time I had become convinced that I would not have recuperated sufficiently by the beginning of the fall term and wanted to let Kathy know about it. I also wanted to ask her to continue covering for me as acting chairman because I was worried that the executive committee member might wish to resume his role in that capacity. Kathy readily agreed to continue and told me not to worry about it. Besides, she informed me, it was premature to make a decision at that time. As I later found out Beatty and Kathy had discussed this issue the night before when I was in the hospital. Kathy later discussed it with the Dean of Arts (she had previously been Associate Dean of Arts).

That night my research assistant and her husband came over to visit me. Marilyn had been my research assistant for about seven years. She was an excellent assistant and highly competent in all aspects of research. I really felt guilty losing my research grant because she was paid out of that grant, but this was tempered by the fact that she and her husband were leaving for Stanford the following week, where he would be spending his sabbatical. It was nice having them visit us. Marilyn had been one of the first people to notice the change in my behavior the winter and spring before, but the only comment she made was that she felt I wasn't spending enough time on my research.

As it got closer and closer to September I became more and more concerned. I was afraid that I would not be able to return to the university and was seriously considering the possibility of going on disability leave. At times I felt I would be an emotional cripple for the rest of my life. I had been depressed so long that I developed a depressive reaction to my depression. I was suffering from a secondary depression.

5

Depression Begets Depression

By mid-August of 1977 I was thoroughly dejected. I had been fighting my depression since the beginning of April and had collapsed at the beginning of June. How long would the depression last? How long? It's true that even if one does nothing about it, depression eventually lifts, but sometimes it can take more than a year. Would this happen to me? None of the medication was helping, I was not getting better spontaneously, and I was becoming even more depressed over the fact that I was still depressed after such a lengthy period. I had developed a secondary depression in reaction to my primary depression.

Secondary Depression

What sort of feelings did I have in July and August? What sort of behavior did I manifest? What difficulties was I having in coping with day-to-day living? It is difficult to put into words how I felt at that time. I guess my major reaction was one of despair—a despair of ever being human again. I honestly felt subhuman, lower than the lowest vermin. Furthermore, I was self-deprecatory and could not understand why anyone would want to associate with me, let alone love me. I became mistrustful and suspicious of others and was certain that they were checking up on me to prove that I was incompetent. What was really frightening was that I felt incompetent myself. Because I could so easily "detect" my own failings, surely all the others who were functioning effectively could easily tell how inadequate I was. This made me

45

anxious and more depressed. In retrospect, I realize that I was developing symptoms of paranoia as part of the depression. I was also becoming paranoid about a number of other functions. These paranoid-like symptoms, which are centered on self-doubt, are frequently a part of the depression; for example, I had become increasingly concerned about finances. On one hand, I thought that I was receiving extra money that I didn't deserve and, on the other, I was certain that we were going bankrupt. In any case, I was positive that I was going to wind up in jail. When I received my July salary statement it appeared to me that the total was larger than it should be. This frightened me and I told my wife that we should phone the university immediately and arrange to return the extra money before I got into trouble. Gently, my wife told me that she thought the amount of money was correct and there was nothing to worry about. Of course, she was right. My statement for July included extra salary for teaching a half-course in Summer School before I became ill.

I was also positive that I was going to be fired from the university because of incompetence and that we would become destitute—that we would go broke. I felt guilty at the prospect of not being able to support my family. Of course, this had no basis in fact. No one was going to fire me. They wouldn't even have put me on disability (something I was looking into). I discovered later that the Dean of Arts and one of the vice-presidents had arranged that even if I stayed away for more than a few months (which, of course, I didn't) I would not be put on disability and would still receive full salary. (I was a charter member of York University and do not know whether that was a factor, but in any case the Dean and the vice-president both thought highly of me and agreed that I was competent.) One certainly has strange and unrealistic thoughts when one is depressed.

Another symptom of paranoia was the feeling that people were checking up on me. At times I was certain that there were some who thought that I was malingering, whereas at others, as indicated earlier, I was certain that they were trying to prove my incompetence. Toward the end of July the Director of the Graduate Programme in Psychology resigned as director and faculty member at York to accept a position as chairman at another university psychology department, effective September 1. If a replacement could not be found, he was willing, although reluctant, to stay on until January. As Chairman of the

Psychology Department at York University I would normally take part in replacing a faculty member and would be on the Search Committee for a Graduate Director. To his credit the executive committee member who was still functioning as acting chairman informed me of the resignation and asked my opinion about what should be done. The first thing we did was to arrange for the graduate director and the acting chairman to come to my house to discuss the matter with me.

The whole matter made me quite anxious and I panicked. Initially, I agreed with the acting chairman who suggested that we insist that the graduate director remain; that is, we should force the graduate director to stay. Because I couldn't at that moment think of a realistic replacement for the graduate director, I tacitly agreed. However, this is never a wise idea for at least two reasons. First, forcing someone to stay against his will creates an uncomfortable and unhealthy atmosphere. Second, no one is indispensable and it is always possible to find a replacement. It was especially unwise in this particular case because one of the major reasons for the abrupt resignation of the graduate director was the difficulty he was experiencing with the faculty and graduate students. The acting chairman arranged to meet the Dean of Arts and I insisted that I go along. I guess I was afraid that they might pull a fast one or make a deal behind my back. At the meeting the Dean, although disturbed by the lateness of the resignation, did not agree that we should force the graduate director to stay. Although I concurred I did not express my agreement. I was still in a fog due to a great extent to my depression. We informed the Dean that we would be meeting that day with the Departmental Executive and Graduate Programme Executive Committees.

On the way to the morning meeting of the Departmental Executive Committee I encountered the Dean of the Faculty of Graduate Studies (a psychologist). The first thing he said to me was, "Norm, what are you doing here? We can handle this matter without you." I misinterpreted the significance of his remarks. He was merely attempting to be solicitous and felt that because I was ill there was no need for me to be bothered by stresses and strains of the meeting. I, of course, considered his remarks as a sign of rejection. He then asked me about my perceptive power and whether things seemed duller to me now than they did before. (A symptom of depression is that one's attention goes awry and one's perception is not so clear and sharp as it is normally.) Because

I thought that he was checking up on me, I replied that my perception was perfectly normal. I was positive that he was attempting to prove that I was incompetent. In fact, he was merely being kind and was concerned about my health and welfare. Oh, paranoia!

During the Departmental Executive Meeting that morning and the Graduate Executive Meeting that afternoon the acting chairman was outvoted and it was agreed that the graduate director be permitted to go and that the department begin a search for a new one. We agreed unanimously on a candidate and asked the Dean of Graduate Studies to determine whether he was willing to serve. The next evening the proposed candidate phoned me at home and told me that he would probably accept the position. It was a nice gesture on his part to keep me informed. He served as graduate director for a two-year period and we all worked very well together. During this whole episode of the resignation and search for a new graduate director I felt inept and "out of it." I guess I hadn't fully accepted the fact that I was ill.

Not only did I feel that the Graduate Dean was trying to prove my incompetence but, I was also certain that the Dean of Art was checking up on me. When he came to visit me again during the third week of August I was positive he was assessing my competence, or lack thereof, and that he was going to fire me. I felt that he had merely tolerated me and that my inadequecies had finally caught up with me. Nothing could be further from the truth. He was genuinely and compassionately concerned about my health. When I at last felt better he told me that I had done an excellent job as chairman and that I was one of the few people on the faculty and in the university capable of doing the Dean's job (his job) as well as or better than he was doing it. So much for my feelings of incompetency and inferiority.

While I had a great deal of time to ruminate, I not only pondered my current situation but my whole career as well. I was positive that I was a fraud and a phony and that I didn't deserve my Ph.D. I didn't deserve to have tenure; I didn't deserve to be a Full Professor; I didn't deserve to be the Chairman of the Psychology Department; I didn't deserve to be a Fellow of the American Psychological Association and the Canadian Psychological Association; I didn't deserve the research grants I had been awarded; I couldn't understand how I had written the books and journal articles that I had and how they had been accepted for publication. I must have conned a lot of people. During this time I continued to denigrate myself. My self-esteem was shot to hell. These are all typical symptoms of depression.

Not only was my self-esteem low with respect to my academic and intellectual achievements but it was low also with respect to my emotional and social life. I analyzed all the people I knew and felt that each of them could do most things better than I could and that each of them had at least one special talent. Of course, in retrospect, all of this seems like patent nonsense, but it was another symptom of depression. I felt extremely dependent on my family and didn't know how I could survive without my wife. How would I cook? How would I wash my clothes? I couldn't even drive a car. I couldn't even get to the doctor by myself. Even if I went by public transportation I would probably get lost. I felt disoriented. I couldn't make up my mind what I should wear or whether to take a shower. I was becoming more and more dependent on my wife and was beginning at times to act like a baby. This terrified me and made me even more depressed. What a dilemma! What could I do?

What would happen if my family deserted me? I recall a time during the end of August when I took the subway with my wife. She had gone through the turnstile before I did and I was positive that she was going to desert me. She probably had had enough of me and my shenanigans and was fed up with my behavior. Of course, nothing could have been further from the truth. Her kindness and devotion, her concern, compassion, and her love, more than anything else, sustained me during my ordeal. If I had to single out the one person who was most instrumental in my getting better, it would be my wife. This is not meant in any way to minimize the accomplishments of Dr. Persad, the psychiatrist whom I saw throughout most of my illness. I will be eternally grateful to both Dr. Persad and my wife. I should be noted also that the strong support that I received from my children was extremely helpful. What is not readily recognized is that the support one receives from one's family is an essential ingredient of the therapeutic process.

Basically, during all this time I felt that I would remain an emotional cripple for the rest of my life. I felt doomed to a state of dependence, misery, and gloom, unable to function properly in my day-to-day living. A number of people asked me if I had ever contemplated suicide. This question is quite in order because suicidal thoughts are frequent during depression and may seem like the only escape from an intolerable situation. Although I thought of suicide in the abstract, because I knew that it was related to depression, I can honestly say, however, that I never thought of it personally as a solution to my ordeal. I probably felt that I was too incompetent even to attempt it. What I thought of was even more frightening, at least to me. I thought that I would remain an emotional cripple. What a prospect! Invariably, I would ask my wife "Do you think that I well ever get better?" I constantly needed assurance and she would try to give it to me. Deep in my heart, however, I was not at all convinced.

In effect, I had gone from denying that I was ill, in the spring, to a conviction that I would never recuperate, in the summer. I was agitated and anxious and had taken to pacing the hall in our home. I was obsessed with my problem. I was whining and demanding and behaved in an "obsessive impulsive" manner. I was suspicious of everyone and trusted no one except my family and Dr. Persad. Each day dragged on endlessly. When one is happy time passes quickly. When one is depressed time passes slowly. Getting up each morning was a hardship—something I dreaded. What would I do with my day? I couldn't plan five minutes ahead but I certainly worried about the future.

Many of these things seem ridiculous and even funny in retrospect, but they certainly were not funny at the time. One humorous incident, which was obviously a manifestation of my paranoid behavior, is in connection with a urine sample that I had to take to the Clarke Institute of Psychiatry. Late in August Dr. Persad, in consultation with Dr. Stancer, recommended that because nothing else was working it would be desirable to administer ECT (electroshock therapy). In preparation for the ECT it was necessary to obtain blood and urine samples and an electrocardiogram (EKG). At this point, I merely wish to tell the story of the urine sample. ECT is discussed in detail in Chapter 7.

I had no trouble producing the urine. The real problem was in finding a bottle in which to store it. As I recall it, quite vividly as a matter of fact, it was a Wednesday night toward the end of August and my daughter was still recuperating from having had her molars removed. My wife looked around the house and the only suitable container she could find was an empty cylindrical medicine bottle that had contained my daughter's antibiotic. I was reluctant to use it because for some reason it was impossible to remove the label completely. It was possible, however, to remove all identifying information. This was not good enough for me. For some reason I was convinced, irrationally, that if I left a sample in that container Dr. Persad would think that it was not my urine sample and would put me in the hospital for lying or that my urine would interact with the remmants (of which there was none) of the previous medication and produce a strange concoction that would not reflect well on me. This too, I believed, would cause me to be hospitalized. I ran around the house refusing to leave the urine sample. This upset everyone in the house and I remember my wife yelling at me. This was probably a kindness on her part to get me back to my senses rather than a burst of anger. At last I found an empty plastic toothpick container and left my urine sample in it.

My behavior was bizarre and paranoid. Not only was I upset myself but I also upset everyone else. One factor that is not sufficiently recognized is that when one is depressed or suffers from some other emotional illness one's behavior is not only personally upsetting but it also causes a great deal of anguish to family and friends. Of course, during the urine caper I was not aware of this. I was preoccupied with myself. During illness, especially during depression, when one regresses and sometimes behaves in an infantile and dependent manner, one also becomes narcissistic. In retrospect, I realize that I was doing just that. It was not intentional. It was merely another manifestation of my illness.

With respect to my medication, I took my pills faithfully more out of paranoia, docility, compliance, and fear than in any belief that they were doing me any good. I was convinced that they were not doing me any good but I continued to hope that they might. Hope springs eternal! There was certainly a reality factor in my perception. I had started on the medication in early June and except for a few weeks had taken the various antidepressants continuously. Here it was the third week in August and nothing much was happening. Of course, it takes about three weeks or so for the antidepressants to have any effect. I had never been on any one of them for three continuous weeks because of the side effects. How could they start having a positive effect?

Why, then, was I taking my medication, especially when the antidepressants produced difficult urination, dryness of mouth, and constipation? It must be noted, however, that all these side effects could be symptoms of my depression. Simply put, it was the plain old paranoia. I was certain that Dr. Persad was keeping track of the number of pills I was taking and would know exactly when I should be asking for a refill of my prescription. Although it is true that physicians keep records of the medication they prescribe, they do not keep detailed accounts of the exact amounts. This would be an impossible task, especially if they were to provide this service for all their patients. I was positive, however, that Dr. Persad had an exact record of how many pills I had left and if I didn't ask for a renewal of the prescription on the right day he would have me hospitalized. Therefore I kept detailed records in my head and even counted the one or two days that I forgot to take my pills. (I remembered the next day but didn't want to compensate by taking extras.) In fact, I was afraid that if I had too many pills and didn't ask for the prescription at the appropriate time my wife would tell Dr. Persad. In addition to all this being a manifestation of paranoia, it also smacks of narcissism on my part. It implies that Dr. Persad had nothing better to do than spend his time worrying about me. I assumed, erroneously, that everything revolved around me.

Another reason that I continued to take my medication was that I trusted Dr. Persad and had faith in the antidepressants. By golly, if he felt that the medication was going to work, it was going to work. It was just a matter of time, eventually they were going to be effective. But my despair was growing with my anguish and agitation.

One of the major reasons for this increase in anxiety was that the way I reckoned it the longer I was ill, the greater the probability that I would be hospitalized. At this stage I became agitated whenever I went to see Dr. Persad, especially in the waiting room, and wanted reassurance from my wife that I would not be hospitalized. In fact, I never was.

Why did I have this morbid fear of hospitalization and was the fear justified? It is my contention that, other than under dire circumstances, a hospital is no place for sick people. It is especially no place for people with an emotional illness. Often times, for a number of reasons, more stresses and strains are created than alleviated in a hospital atmosphere. For the most part, all of us are creatures of habit and to a fair extent have control of what we do. We encounter the same people from day to day and can predict their behavior; they, in turn, can predict ours. When there is a disruption in our daily routine, except when we seek out something different, we are likely to become irritable. This is not to say that we do not enjoy surprises, but if the disruptive activities are too dissonant with our expectations we are wont to become anxious.

Basically, what being in a hospital, especially in a psychiatric hospital, means is going from close family interaction to close interaction with other patients and staff. There is a certain loss of privacy; a certain loss of individuality. From pretty much choosing your comings and goings you are at the mercy of the medical and paramedical staff. Then there are pressures from the other patients; you have to put up with their idiosyncracies and they have to put up with yours. You cannot be alone when you choose to be but must observe the hospital routine. Rules and regulations become important determinants of your behavior. It involves adjustment to a new environment at a time when you are having the greatest difficulty coping with the old.

In addition to the reality factors and fears associated with being hospitalized, a number of others had an effect on me. To me it seemed like going to prison. I was afraid that I would be labeled insane and that would mean the end of my career. I wondered whether the other patients would consider me incompetent, dependent, and helpless. I felt that it would put me in an awkward situation because some of our graduate students were interning or doing their practicum work at the Clarke Institute of Psychiatry. At home I was in a protected environment, whereas in the hospital I would be subjected to the whims and foibles of the other patients, the rules of the hospital, and to some extent the whims of the staff.

There may, however, be positive aspects to a stay in the hospital. Some people may prefer and need its more structured environment and may find it more protective. Patients in the hospital have more immediate access to professional help than those who remain at home. The change of scenery that the hospital provides can be helpful to some. If the family is having difficulty caring for the patient at home, hospitalization may reduce the strain on its members. In some instances part of the problem lies in the interaction of patient and family. Sometimes the home environment is a poor one and not conducive to easy recovery. For some people hospitalization is the best solution.

Probably two or three factors saved me from being hospitalized. First, I had the strong support, protection, and care of my family and therefore was able to manage well enough. Second, I was in touch with reality (although at times I had a somewhat distorted view of reality), and, third I was in no way dangerous to myself or others. Furthermore, I had good resources and the prognosis was quite good. Everyone recovers from depression eventually. I cannot really understand how depressed people without family support can survive without being hospitalized. Family support is the *sine qua non* for the treatment of depression.

One other reaction which developed at that time occurred after I had started taking the Aventyl(nortriptyline). I developed a funny metallic taste in my mouth and felt as if my gums were rotting. I truly felt that I had jungle mouth. I was certain that it was in reaction to the Aventyl and to this day don't really know whether it was. I had never had this reaction to any of the other drugs, which may have been exacerbated by my pipe which I was smoking more heavily than usual. (I have since stopped smoking.) I wasn't cleaning my pipe properly and it developed a foul smell. I was beyond caring, however, and was not too perturbed by the way my mouth felt. I did make a point, however, of keeping clean personally. I showered every day, wore clean clothes every day, and brushed my teeth twice a day. I must admit, however, that I ceased to floss my teeth.

In retrospect it is surprising that although I did not give a damn about myself I was still concerned about good grooming, but I did refuse to get new clothes. My wife wanted me to buy a new summer suit which was on sale. I refused by saying "What do I need it for; I'm not going anywhere and will be staying in doors. It's a waste of money." After a while she stopped arguing with me and treated it as a lost cause. Obviously, I would rather sit around the house all day and mope than go out. I did manage, however, to go for a walk every day or two.

In general, the excuse I gave for my inactivity was fatigue—extreme sometimes to the point of exhaustion. I was too tired to make decisions and felt as if I had a huge weight on my back that wouldn't allow me to achieve anything. Had anyone told me I would ever feel this way I wouldn't have believed it. It's just inconceivable and one cannot really appreciate the feeling unless one has experienced it. No matter how long I stayed in bed and slept I never felt rested and refreshed. I had difficulty falling asleep and even more waking up. When I did get out of bed I was lethargic. I was as slow as molasses.

The longer my illness lasted the guiltier I became. In many ways I felt like a parasite. All I did was eat and sleep, talk to people when they visited, and go for walks. I couldn't read nor even concentrate on watching television. I couldn't prepare the grill to barbeque steaks or hamburgers. I couldn't concentrate long enough to rake the lawn.

Furthermore, I was bored, bored, bored—bored silly. Through all this, through thick and thin, my wife and children stood by me without complaining and with a tremendous show of emotional support. My son tried to encourage me to play tennis with him and I did go out once during the summer, but my performance was pathetic and this made me feel even worse. My coordination was awful. Possibly the medication was a contributing factor.

My son, who was about to begin his third year at the University of Toronto, had planned to move downtown with some of his friends. This was perfectly natural. He was 20 years old and wanted to be on his own and being downtown would be closer to the campus and to the excitement of the city, but I had become dependent on him and couldn't bear the prospect of the separation, even though I would see him often. It is always difficult for parents when their children leave home (even though they may not admit it). This situation was exacerbated by my illness. I was also overly concerned about the extra cost and was certain that I couldn't afford it (even though my son was planning to pay part of his own expenses). I was almost in tears and begged him to stay at home. I was also concerned about how my wife could care for me with only my daughter to support her. I felt quite strongly that my wife also needed the help of my son. He was obviously dismayed by my request to delay his departure because he had planned to move in with his friends who had already rented a house. Nevertheless, after thinking about it for a few days he decided to remain, much to my relief. He moved the following May with my blessing and encouragement. The separation anxiety was minimal and we see him quite frequently. He and I are on best of terms, for I believe that our relationship was strengthened by his selfless behavior.

Every little thing irritated me. My daughter had wanted to adopt two baby rats as pets. I flew into a temper and became quite agitated. She really wanted them, for if she did not take them from her friend's sister they would be put away. This didn't bother me. I was concerned only that I would be inconvenienced. I had some support from my son, who was not too enthusiastic about having the rats around. My wife felt that my daughter should have them, but I really carried on. After about a month my wife insisted that we accept the rats and I was too tried to argue with her any more. As it turned out the prospect was worse than the reality. My daughter looked after them, with the help of my wife (my son and I refused even to touch them) and they did not bother me at all.

Toward the end of August, when I still had made no progress and was becoming concerned about being hospitalized, Dr. Persad gave me a choice between ECT and hospitalization as a course of treatment. He stated that if I were to be hospitalized it would be at Homewood, in Guelph, which is about 50 miles from Toronto, and not at the Clarke Institute. He was concerned that too many people knew me at the Clarke and that there was a chance that my treatment would be compromised because of my standing in the profession. There might also be some stigma if I were at the Clarke. It was my guess that he favored ECT, but he knew about my strong negative attitudes toward it, and it is entirely possible that by suggesting hospitalization he nudged me toward a decision to undergo ECT. He said that he wanted Beatty and me to make the decision. Some decision. Out of the frying pan and into the fire! I reluctantly chose ECT (in retrospect a wise step) as the lesser of two evils. ECT and its social, political, and personal implications are discussed in Chapter 7.

The behavior that I exhibited at that time was not unique to me. It is fairly characteristic of most people suffering from depression. They illustrate the symptoms that I described in Chapter 2 and provide a clear-cut example of the major affective disorders discussed more formally and systematically in Chapter 10. Although at this time I had been diagnosed as having a unipolar (endogenous) depression, as described in Chapter 8, I actually had a bipolar (manic-depressive) affective (endogenous) disorder. For a technical and scientific description of the various affective disorders and their causes and for a discussion of the various theories of depression the reader is referred to Chapter 10.

6

Of Drugs and Wings and Many Things

This chapter relates the history of antidepressant drugs—how they were discovered, how they operate, and when they are indicated. Basically, there are two major types of antidepressant, the tricyclics and monoamine oxidase (MAO) inhibitors. This chapter discusses the more technical aspects of drugs and Chapter 7 describes electroconvulsive therapy (ECT), an alternative treatment for depression.

Psychopharmacology or drug therapy for the affective disorders and other emotional problems began early in the Christian era. Charak Sastra Charka, a Hindu physician, administered herbal drugs in the treatment of depression during the first century A.D. As early as the second century A.D. Chinese physicians used opiate derivatives to treat depression. Bleuler, the psychiatrist, used tincture of opium for depression in 1924, and for a few years in the mid-1880s Freud took cocaine to deal with his depressive moods. Even earlier, Hippocrates, the Greek physician, in the fourth century B.C. used hot spring baths in the north of Italy that contained lithium salts in the treatment of manic-depression. Various psychomotor stimulants such as amphetamine and methylphenidate were used for short periods to treat depression before the recent development of antidepressant drugs. Furthermore, hormones like estrogen and Acth were also administered for a brief period between 1950 and 1955. In all this time, however, electroshock therapy (ECT) was the most effective treatment for depression.

The third revolution in the treatment of mental illness (the first being the unshackling of inmates by Pinel and Pussin, the second, Freudian psychoanalysis) is based on the antidepressant drugs developed in the

1950s. The discovery that the tricyclic and monoamine oxidase inhibitor drugs were effective in the treatment of depression was serendipitous.

Imipramine (trade name Tofranil), the first of the tricyclic drugs used with success in the treatment of depression, was administered by Roland Kuhn and his colleagues in 1956 at the Cantonal Psychiatric Clinic in Münsterlingen, Switzerland. These scientists were attempting to find a useful antischizophrenia drug. (Imipramine had been synthesized and chemically described in 1899 by Thiele and Holzinger.) Kuhn found that the medication, then known as G22, 355, was not particularly successful in treating schizophrenia. However, he and his colleagues noted that the depressed schizophrenics became less depressed.

In three well-designed studies conducted with depressed patients it was revealed that imipramine had antidepressant characteristics. Roland Kuhn presented the results of his studies at the Second International Congress of Psychiatry in Zurich on September 6, 1957, to a grand audience of about one dozen persons. Although Kuhn's paper was received with particular interest, a certain degree of skepticism was evident. There were two reasons for this. First, up to that time drugs had not been effective in treating depression. Second, Kuhn's final conclusions were based on only 40 carefully examined cases. The first publication on imipramine (authored by Kuhn) appeared in the Swiss Medical Journal, dated August 31, 1957. In the 1960s a few million patients were given imipramine and about 5000 reports were published on its effects. Furthermore, at least 40 to 50 other tricyclic antidepressants (in 10 chemical classes) have been synthesized and investigated. In general, the tricyclics are especially effective in the treatment of unipolar and bipolar (endogenous) depression.

1956 was a vintage year for the discovery of the antidepressant drugs. Not only did Roland Kuhn and his colleagues develop the first of the tricyclic drugs (imipramine) but Nathan Kline, a psychiatrist at Rockland State Hospital in New York, found that iproniazid, a drug designed to treat tuberculosis, induced a state of elation and increased alertness in tubercular patients. (This drug was introduced by Bernheim in 1928.) Kline administered it to depressed patients and noted that it had antidepressant properties. Iproniazid (or Marsilid, its trade name) was the first of the monoamine oxidase (MAO) inhibitor antidepressant drugs. Kline called this drug a psychic energizer. The tricyclics and

MAO inhibitors are the two standard types of antidepressant drug in use today. (John F. Cade's discovery in Australia in 1949 that lithium had therapeutic effects against mania was also serendipitous.)

How do these antidepressants work? When are they indicated and when are they contraindicated? There is sufficient evidence today to indicate that the prime physiological cause of the unipolar and bipolar affective disorders (depression and manic-depression) is a chemical imbalance. Although the role of biological and genetic factors is strongly implicated in the etiology of the affective disorders, we cannot at the moment offer a precise conclusion with respect to the cause of these illnesses. Therefore the influence of psychological and social factors should not be ignored.

In 1953, a few years before the discovery of the effectiveness of imipramine and MAO inhibitors for the treatment of depression, a new drug was introduced for treating high blood pressure, or hypertension. Side effects of the antihypertensive drug were drowsiness, withdrawal, and depression in many of the patients who took it. This drug was Reserpine, which was derived or extracted from *Rauwolfia Serpentina*, a genus of herbs. In Hindu medicine *Rauwolfia* was used to treat stomach ulcers, fever, snakebite, complications of pregnancy, and high blood pressure and as an agent for calming the mentally ill. *Rauwolfia* also functions effectively as a sedative. Nathan Kline, who was then chiefly interested in schizophrenia, gave *Rauwolfia* to hospitalized patients in a mental hospital.

Reserpine (*Rauwolfia*), administered initially for hypertension, produced depression; the MAO inhibitors, administered initially for tuberculosis, produced euphoria or hypomania. These findings have important implications for depression and the manic-depressive cycle. Dr. Nathan Kline was involved in researching both drugs and Dr. Roland Kuhn investigated the tricyclics. The MAO inhibitors and the tricyclics are the drug, of choice in the treatment of depression. Reserpine, although used primarily with schizophrenics, was used to treat hypomania until the advent of lithium. The discovery that these drugs are highly effective in the treatment of the affective disorders was primarily serendipitous. Their value stems from the possible link between the affective disorders and the biochemistry of the body. Empirical evidence suggests a relationship between changes in the catecholamine metabolism of the central nervous system and the affective disorders.

Norepinephrine (noradrenaline), which is produced in the body and is related to activation and arousal, is relevant to our affective and behavioral states. When depletion and/or inactivation of norepinephrine occurs the result is sedation or depression. When there is an increase or potentiation of norepinephrine, the result is excitement and stimulation. Therefore drugs that can deplete or diminish norepinephrine and/or epinephrine should produce depression and those that can increase norepinephrine and/or epinephrine should produce elation. The brain regulates the production and distribution of norepinephrine and/or epinephrine.

It is necessary to say something here about the brain, about how nerves work, and about neural transmission. The brain consists of tens of billions of nerve cells called neurons.

The neurons communicate with one another across gaps or junctions called synapses, via the release of chemicals called neurotransmitters. About 20 of them have been discovered. The neural transmission can be presented schematically.

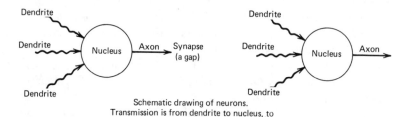

Schematic drawing of neurons.
Transmission is from dendrite to nucleus, to
axon, across the synapse to the next cell.

As it crosses the synapse (which is a gap) between two neurons (or nerve cells), the electrical message transforms into a chemical carrier or neurotransmitter. This neurotransmitter fits into the receptor of the next neuron and then reverts to an electrical message. All neurotransmitters and chemicals (including drugs) that copy neurotransmitters operate like keys in a lock. They fit only into those nerve receptors that are especially constituted to accept them; that is, a "round" neurotransmitter cannot fit or be accepted by a "square" nerve receptor.

The evidence seems to indicate that when the brain produces too many or too few chemicals, such as the catecholamines, one of the results is an emotional disturbance; for example, depression is related to extremely low levels of a family of catecholamines called the monoamines (namely dopamine, noradrenaline, and adrenaline). These monoamines can be destroyed by the enzyme monoamine oxidase (MAO). The MAO inhibitor drugs prevent the enzyme from destroying the monoamines, and the tricyclic antidepressant drugs function by prolonging the longevity of the monoamines in the synapse. The three catecholamines determine a person's capability of experiencing such moods as alertness, pleasure, satisfaction, happiness, drive, and desire. Serotonin, a fourth neurotransmitter, belongs to a different chemical family, namely, the indoleamines, and is also related to depressive disorders. There may be other neurotransmitters related to the affective disorders.

The catecholamine neurons total about one million cells of a total of more than 10 billion in the neocortex alone. Therefore they constitute only a small fraction of the total. Their influence and effect, however, are highly disproportionate to their number. They serve broad and diffuse networks of neural pathways and have a profound effect on mood and emotion.

Basically, the brain operates in terms of stimuli and responses. Physical stimuli emanate continuously from various parts of the body to the brain and impart information relevant to vision, hearing, smell, taste, touch, and pain. The stimuli travel along the nerve fibers and across the synapse to the next cell. This continues until the message or signal reaches the brain; for example, if you put your hand on a hot stove, a pain signal travels to your brain, which then analyzes the stimulus and responds in terms of "get that hand away from the hot stove." This occurs reflexively. The stimulus, the perception of pain, and the response all occur almost simultaneously.

Sometimes, however, the system breaks down. Sometimes the signals do not get through. Sometimes the signals are weakened, sometimes strengthened. Sometimes they get through too quickly, sometimes too slowly; for example, if you have an anaesthetic injected into your gums for dental work, you will not feel the dentist's probe or drill. The message of pain is not getting through to the brain.

Similarly, stimuli or signals relevant to emotions may not get through to the brain. A happy situation transmits a stimulus or signal and normally the response is a cheerful one. A threatening situation transmits a stimulus or signal and normally the response is one of fear or anxiety. There are stimuli and responses and there are relevant moods.

We usually feel better when the sun is shining than when it is raining. What happens when something goes wrong with the connections? Why does a depressed person react unhappily to a bright and sunny day? Why can a manic person laugh in reaction to a frightening situation, such as a flood, earthquake, or thunderstorm?

Objectively, a situation may appear to be conducive to joy, yet the depressed individual seems sad. You tell a depressed person that he has won an award and all you get in return is a blank stare. What has gone wrong? Perhaps there is a breakdown in the metabolism of the catecholamines.

As indicated earlier, there appears to be a link between manic-depressive disorders and changes in the metabolism of catecholamines in the central nervous system. The neurotransmitters pass the signals along to various parts of the brain with respect to mood or affect. They help to regulate mood. If insufficient numbers of neurotransmitters get through the system, if they are out of balance, our emotional responses will be inadequate and inappropriate.

We do not know specifically which of the catecholamine neurons mediate or transmit the emotions or how they do it. We do know that there are neurons that mediate mood, that affect our emotions and behavior. It is extremely difficult to localize the chemical compounds and to investigate the functions of the brain. The synapse can be seen only with an extremely powerful microscope; it cannot be "touched" directly. The amounts of catecholamine fluids transmitted at the synapse are minute. The only way we presently have of assessing levels of the catecholamines is by blood, urine, and spinal fluid samples in which tiny amounts of the neurotransmitters are excreted.

Research has shown that changes in noradrenaline (or norepinephrine) metabolism are related to mood changes. Low levels of noradrenaline excretion occur during periods of depression, high levels during periods of hypomania, and moderate levels during normal moods. Note, however, that noradrenaline is not necessarily reduced in all kinds of depression.

The evidence seems to be fairly conclusive that unipolar depression and the depressive phase of the bipolar affective disorders are related to deficiences in the catecholamines (primarily noradrenaline) and serotonin in the synapse. Reserpine reduces the availability of noradrenaline and serotonin in the synapse. Evidence of this comes from continuous monitoring and assessment of the levels of noradrenaline and serotonin in the blood, urine, and cerebrospinal fluids. When patients are depressed their noradrenaline and serotonin levels are lower than when their moods are normal.

An excess of noradrenaline at the synapse leads to hypomania or euphoria. Evidence of this comes from an assessment of noradrenaline levels in the urine, blood, and cerebrospinal fluids. During hypomania there is an increase in noradrenaline.

Kline's research on reserpine and iproniazid, plus Roland Kuhn's research on imipramine, led to the development of the two major classes of antidepressant drug: the tricyclics and the MAO inhibitors. Both operate on a basis that is opposite to that of the effects produced by Reserpine; that is, they increase the amount of noradrenaline (and in some instances serotonin) in the synapse area.

The MAO inhibitors and the tricyclics increase the supply of the catecholamines (primarily noradrenaline) in two different ways.

MAO Inhibitors

An enzyme called monoamine oxidase serves to arrest the production of noradrenaline in the area of the synapse, beyond an optimum level. This keeps the biochemical system in proper balance. There is reason to believe that for (biochemically) depressed persons too little noradrenaline is produced or too much noradrenaline is rendered inactive by the monoamine oxidase. The result is a diminution in the supply of noradrenaline, followed by depression. The MAO inhibitors work by inhibiting the inhibitors and therefore allow more noradrenaline to be produced and to fire across the synapse.

There are two main subgroups of the MAO inhibitors: hydrazine (trade name Nardil) and nonhydrazine (trade name Parnate). Both MAO inhibitors are quickly and easily absorbed in the gastrointestinal tract when taken orally. Plasma concentration of the drug reaches its peak in one to three hours after ingestion.

Today the MAO inhibitors are used primarily to treat depression, phobias, anxiety states, and narcolepsy (a frequent and uncomfortable need for short periods of deep sleep). They are used rarely today for treating hypertension and ulcers. Both Parnate and Nardil should be administered under strict supervision because of the possibility of toxic reactions caused by the interaction of these drugs with a substance called tyramine contained in certain foods (e.g., herring, sour cream, chicken livers, cheese, and chocolate), drink (e.g., wine and hard liquor), and certain drugs (e.g., narcotics, barbiturates, alcohol, and tricyclics). Because of their possible toxicity, it is advisable to try the MAO inhibitors only if the depression does not respond to the tricyclic drugs or if for some reason electroconvulsive treatment (ECT) is contraindicated.

Tricyclic Antidepressants

The tricyclic class of drugs, unlike the MAO inhibitors, operates directly on the transmission of noradrenaline in the synapse. Normally some noradrenaline is reabsorbed into the neuron from the synapse. If too much is reabsorbed or too little is emitted into the synapse, there is a deficiency of noradrenaline—a depletion of neurotransmission—and as a result depression may occur. The tricyclic antidepressants block or slow down the reabsorption of noradrenaline into the neuron and the amount of an active neurotransmitter (i.e., noradrenaline) in the synapse is elevated. As a consequence, after about two or three weeks of medication the depressive symptoms will be alleviated.

Usually the tricyclic drugs are preferred to the MAO inhibitors as antidepressants, because, as indicated earlier, the MAO inhibitors can have potentially dangerous side effects and usually necessitate dietary restrictions for those persons taking the pills.

Since about 1956 10 different chemical classes of tricyclic antidepressant drug have been discovered and synthesized. At present, only three of them are available in Canada. The tricyclic antidepressants are chemically similar to the phenothiazines, which have been used in treating schizophrenia, but they are not identical.

The tricyclic drugs are effective in treating depression because they potentiate the transmission of catecholamines (noradrenaline) and indoleamines (serotonin) across the synapses. Depression can also be induced by drugs like reserpine, digitalis, and L-Dopa. The tricyclics are the most frequently used antidepressants. They are also effective, therapeutically, for tantrums, school phobias in children, nocturnal enuresis, phobias, and obsessive and compulsive neuroses.

As indicated earlier, the tricyclics usually take two to three weeks to produce results. If the initial drug doesn't work, the psychiatrist will try another and another until he may resort to ECT. Recent research by Dr. David Kupfer, a psychiatrist at the Western Psychiatric Institute and Clinic in Pittsburgh, indicates that even when there is no obvious change in the patient's mood and emotions the drug almost instantaneously delays the onset of dreaming. It is well known that depressed persons have difficulty falling asleep and tend to wake up early. Furthermore, they fall into an intense period of sleep, characterized by rapid eye movements (REM), much earlier than normal people. The tricyclic drugs reset the REM sleep clock back to normal even before the symptoms of depression disappear. They also delay the onset of dreaming. Dr. Kupfer has suggested that REM could be instrumental in terms of finding the most appropriate therapeutic drug or by identifying patients for ECT, especially those for whom the tricyclics do not work.

Rarely are the side effects of tricyclic antidepressants severe. Those that may occur are dryness of mouth, flushing, sweating, hypotension (usually), hypertension (rarely), palpitation, itching, rashes, nausea, diarrhea, constipation, heartburn, appetite increase, weight gain, mild headaches, dizzyness, numbness, blurred vision, restlessness, confusion, hypomania, urinary retention. Not all of them occur in everyone and those that do attenuate after a few weeks on the drug. Although the drugs are not addictive, a sudden and abrupt cessation of medication can produce nausea, vomiting, headaches, irritability, and the jitters. The reader will recall (see Chapter 4) that I became irritable, tense, jittery, hypomanic and then "collapsed" into depression when because of urinary reactions I suddenly stopped taking the antidepressant tricyclic.

The tricyclics do not mix well with alcohol because drugs and alcohol potentiate one another and may produce drowsiness and dizziness. Drugs also do not interact well with barbiturates. Furthermore, one should not drive for a few hours after taking 75 mg or more of the antidepressants. These antidepressants are also considered unsafe during pregnancy, especially during the first three months. The tricyclics and MAO inhibitors should not be used simultaneously.

Are the antidepressants effective in combatting depression? In general, the answer is a resounding yes. A review of the research literature from the late 1950s to the early 1970s indicates that in comparison to placebos antidepressants are effective in alleviating depression in two of every three cases (67 percent of the time). More specifically, with the pooling of the results of 23 published placebo-controlled studies it was found that 65 percent of 550 patients showed an overall improvement with imipramine, but only 21 percent of 459 patients showed improvement with an inactive placebo. Later studies showed 70 percent overall improvement in 734 patients on imipramine, contrasted to 39 percent overall improvement in 606 patients on a placebo. Similar results have been found for the other antidepressants. At present there is no evidence to indicate that any one tricyclic antidepressant drug is more effective than another. There is evidence, however, to indicate that the overall effectiveness of the tricyclics is superior to that of the MAO inhibitors. Nevertheless, ECT appears to produce a quicker and more radical effect than the tricyclics. It is possible that ECT potentiates the transmission of noradrenaline into the synapse and affects the metabolism of the catecholamines.

Lithium

If the late 1950s and 1960s belong to the antidepressants as the treatment of choice for affective disorders, the 1970s and 1980s may well belong to lithium. It should be noted that lithium is one of the elements of the periodic table. Lithium, which is used in treating manic-depressive disorders, is related chemically to calcium, magnesium, potassium, and sodium. All of these four salts occur naturally in the human body and all participate in various physiological and biochemical processes. Possibly lithium works by replacing or displacing calcium, magnesium, potassium, and/or sodium, or it may be that lithium functions in a manner opposite that of the tricyclics. It may slow down the release, and increase the reabsorption, of noradrenaline. In general, it is used in the first instance to bring someone down from a high or hypomanic to a more normal state. It serves as a prophylactic for depression. Perhaps it produces a "fine tuning" of our affective states.

In addition to seeing Dr. Persad, my initial course of treatment consisted of, the tricyclics (amitriptyline) plus a tranquilizer. When this didn't work out, because of the side effects, I was shifted to the MAO inhibitors. I was then shifted to the nortriptyline tricyclics (Aventyl) because of the hypertension crisis, and when this was ineffective I was given ECT. The next chapter discusses the "bugaboo" of electroconvulsive or electroshock therapy.

7
Living Better Electrically

The most controversial and probably the most effective method of treating depression is ECT. To a great extent this controversy was dramatically fueled by Ken Kesey's 1962 novel *One Flew Over the Cuckoo's Nest* and by the subsequent movie made from it. In that novel, McMurphy, the tough, freewheeling, gambling "hero," inappropriately receives ECT in a mental institution as a means of calming him down, a method for making him less boisterous. The misuses of ECT have poisoned the public's attitude toward it. Just because automobiles kill more than 50,000 people a year in the United States doesn't mean that we should stop using them. Similarly, just because ECT has been misused or used carelessly and sometimes indiscriminately does not mean that it lacks a proper place in the treatment of the affective disorders.

When did it all begin? When did the practice of administering electricity to the heads of patients with emotional problems start? At first blush it does not seem like the most obvious treatment, but nevertheless it has existed for a number of centuries; for example, electric eels were applied to the head until electric generators were discovered in the eighteenth century. (The electric stimulus from the torpedo fish relieved headaches in A.D. 43.)

Some physicians in the eighteenth and nineteenth centuries had remarkable faith in the electric-eel and electric-generator treatments. They claimed that these methods were successful in treating mentally ill patients. In the present century the level of electric current was raised sufficiently to produce convulsions.

Convulsions have also been induced by chemical means and there have been nonconvulsive chemical treatments as well. In 1922 Dr. Jakob Klaesi used barbiturates and various other chemicals to induce sleep for periods as long as a week. His goal was to allow the nervous system to rest, a procedure that was quite effective for those patients who were severely agitated.

The first chemically induced convulsion occurred in 1785. Oliver treated mental illness by inducing convulsions by administering large doses of camphor. This method was revived about 1933 in Hungary by Dr. Ladislas von Meduna, who injected camphor oil intramuscularly into schizophrenics to produce convulsions. There were two reasons why this treatment was tried. First, it had been observed for some time that the symptoms of patients would disappear after a spontaneous convulsion, independent of the etiology of the convulsion. Second, there was evidence to indicate that epilepsy (involving convulsive seizures) and schizophrenia rarely, if ever, occurred in the same patient. It is ironic to note, as discovered later, that the best results with convulsive therapy were not with schizophrenia but with the affective disorders. Von Meduna changed from camphor oil to induce convulsions to a synthetic preparation called Metrazol (pentylenetetrazol). The intravenous injection of Metrazol produced convulsions more reliably. During this same period (1931–1933) Dr. Manfred Sakel found that the injection of insulin induced a physiological coma which improved brain functioning, especially in schizophrenics.

After the time of von Meduna and Sakel many other drugs were tried for convulsive therapy. At present, however, only one drug, called Indoklon (which is the trade name for the chemical hexafluorodiethyl ether), is still, although rarely, used. In 1956 Krantz, a pharmacologist, and Kurland, a clinician, introduced the inhalant Indoklon, which produced convulsions. At first Indoklon was not readily accepted as a somatic therapy because of the increased cost, the awkwardness of the technique (originally intravenous, now inhaled), and because ECT was considered a more satisfactory technique by most clinicians. However, a number of psychiatrists persisted in using it, techniques for administering it were improved, and in the last few years more widespread uses and research have been related to it. Incidentally, the word Indoklon is derived from the Latin *inducere* (to induce) and the Greek *klonos* (meaning intense movement). Indoklon is a stable, nonflammable, colorless liquid with the odor of ether and a mild anesthetic effect.

The three procedures of prolonged sleep (Klaesi), chemical convulsions (von Meduna), and insulin coma (Sakel) were later modified and perfected. As indicated earlier, except for limited applications of Indoklon to produce convulsions, other chemical methods are rarely used. The Japanese combined prolonged rest and sleep as a form of treatment for the mentally ill, but it was not necessarily produced chemically. Von Meduna's chemical convulsive method is effective in that it led, after much refinement, to present-day electroconvulsive (electroshock) or electrical stimulation therapy, commonly known as ECT.

Electroshock Therapy

In 1938 Ugo Cerletti and Lucio Bini of Italy substituted electrically induced for chemically (or pharmacologically) induced convulsions. They were the first to use electricity in this capacity and gave the treatment the name "electroshock therapy" (ECT). This was an unfortunate choice for it is actually a misnomer. The term electric stimulation would have been much more appropriate. ECT is now part of the common language and we use it here. It does *not* produce a physiological, psychological, or surgical shock. It is not traumatic. It is probably the most effective method of treating the affective disorders. The present methods are very safe!

Cerletti and Bini, in their original publication in 1938, used the basic Italian term *l'elettroshock,* which simply means "the electric stimulus." Dr. Cerletti, in a later article (1950), apologized for this word because of its unfortunate implications, but by then it was too late because the terminology "shock treatments" had pervaded the medical language and titillated the scared fantasies of many people, particularly the insecure. Because the method of treatment was so successful, psychiatrists did not feel obligated to do anything about the upsetting effect of the word *electroshock.*

For people "in the know" ECT is the treatment of choice of many moderate depressions and for all severe ones. Many psychiatrists I have spoken to have informed me that if they were depressed the treatment they would choose for themselves would be ECT. Clinical studies have shown that ECT is the most reliable, effective, and convenient technique for alleviating disabling and/or intense depression. Unfortunately, much of the knowledge about ECT comes to the layman in magazine articles, fiction, movies, or television; for example, the January 1980 issue of the *Atlantic Monthly* has an article by Fred Hapgood on ECT with the scarcely objective title "Electroshock: The Unkindest Therapy of All." The negative tone of the article is well reflected by its title. In *One Flew Over the Cuckoo's Nest* Ken Kesey describes electroshock as "a device that might be said to do the work of the sleeping pill, the electric chair, *and* the torture rack." Sylvia Plath, in her novel *The Bell Jar* vividly describes her perceptions of ECT:

> Then something bent down and took hold of me and shook me like the end of the world. Whee-ee-ee-ee, it shrilled, through an air with crackling blue light, and with each flash a great jolt drubbed me till I thought my bones would break and the sap fly out of me like a split plant. I wondered what terrible thing it was that I had done.

Fred Hapgood quotes the above statement from Sylvia Plath's *The Bell Jar* in his *Atlantic Monthly* article on ECT. In *One Flew Over the Cuckoo's Nest,* Ken Kesey presents ECT in a setting of *gothic horror*. The type of journalistic and dramatic sensationalism, which bears little resemblance to the present-day facts, has greatly contributed to society's negative attitudes toward ECT. This "scare them" approach is both inexcusable and irresponsible. Hapgood's quoting Sylvia Plath's terrifying statement is equivalent to discussing the pain and suffering of surgery without benefit of anesthesia. Any novelist or journalist can easily verify by visiting a hospital or psychiatrist's office, where it is administered, that ECT is not a gothic horror tale. It is a humane treatment. Sensationalism is no substitute for the facts.

ECT: The Past and the Present.   ECT is basically effective because it induces a convulsion and not because of the methodology used. As a function of research and ensuing time it has become a highly sophisticated technique. Currently it is neither a traumatic nor an unpleasant treatment.

The first machine for administering ECT, by alternating current, was built by Lucio Bini. Although many changes have been incorporated since 1938, most ECT machines are derived from and based on the model that Bini built. The basic technique, devised by Cerletti and Bini, consisted of electrodes that were applied to both temples. The amount of alternating electrical current applied ranged from 70 to 130 volts for a duration of 0.1 to 0.6 second and occasionally even 1 second. The slow and steady increase in the current, called the "glissando" technique by Teitz, is believed to have reduced the possibility of fractures. The original treatments were unpremedicated. The shock was administered and convulsions occurred. Later on, sedatives and anticonvulsive drugs were given to diminish the intensity of the convulsions. At times curare preparations were used, but they produced prolonged apnea (asphyxia) and frequent fatalities. During the early days of ECT it was often horrific.

My first contact with ECT will provide the "flavor" of the general atmosphere surrounding it and will also help to explain why I had such a strong negative attitude toward it. During the mid-to-late 1950s I was a graduate student in clinical psychology at the University of Illinois. As part of our training we were required to study various clinical techniques and procedures which included ECT. We visited a psychiatric state hospital in central Illinois to observe patients of various diagnostic categories and how ECT was administered.

As I write this, I still shudder at the memory and still feel the sickness in my stomach. Fortunately, the procedures are now much more humane and benevolent. The patient then was wheeled into the room in his bed, lying on his back. We were in an observation room a few yards away. In addition to the doctor and the nurse, four attendants were present. The ECT machine and a wash basin were the only equipment in the room. Otherwise, it was bare. No anesthetic was to be administered, but it is possible that some oxygen was available, but I do not recall seeing it. The four attendants pinned the patient down to prevent injury during the procedure. Electrodes were pasted on both temples and the shock was administered. A series of convulsions occurred and the patient emitted a blood-curdling yell. I believe the force of the shock broke his back. I was revolted. I felt queasy and faint and couldn't speak. I turned around and left the room. The impression of that scene that occurred more than twenty-five years ago has never left me. That was in 1955. During the intervening years I refused again and again to observe the administration of ECT. I made fun of it and downgraded it. I made puns about it, called it "revolting," and accused numerous psychiatrists of getting a "charge" out of it. I could not discuss it rationally. My psychiatric colleagues tried to explain to me that the techniques had changed, that muscle relaxants and anesthetics were administered in conjunction with the shock treatment, that ECT was now usually administered unilaterally rather than bilaterally, and that memory loss was rare. I countered by showing them articles written in opposition to it. Most of my psychological colleagues had negative attitudes that were no different from mine. We were all biased and prejudiced and refused to accept the new techniques.

In late August 1977 when it was suggested that I consider ECT as a possible course of treatment for my depression I was repelled. The alternatives were hospitalization or the misery of depression, both of which were highly repugnant to me. But hospitalization, especially in a strange town (Homewood, in Guelph, as indicated earlier) was more repugnant than ECT. At that time I was so desperate that if Dr. Persad had suggested that walking down Yonge Street (the main street in Toronto) nude would be beneficial to me I probably would have done it. Therefore I agreed, although reluctantly, to ECT as a course of treatment for my depression.

Knowing my negative attitudes, concern, agitation, and anxiety, Dr. Persad was careful to explain what the treatment involved. He reassured me that the treatment would be done on an outpatient basis and that I would be given a physical examination, a general anesthetic, and a muscle relaxant (and therefore would feel nothing). I would also be required to sign a consent form, which I did on the day that I took the various physical tests. After a few minutes reflection my wife and I agreed on ECT as the course of action. I believe that this was on Tuesday, August 30, I was to return on Thursday, September 1, for the EKG, blood, urine, and blood pressure tests, and the ECT would begin on Friday, September 2. Dr. Persad informed me that 6 to 12 sessions would be required and that they would occur on Mondays, Wednesdays, and Fridays at eight in the morning. I was told not to eat anything or to take any medication after midnight on the evening before a treatment because an anesthetic was to be given. I was also told to bring my pajamas, robe, and slippers.

My wife's attitude toward ECT was similar to mine. This was really because she had formed her opinion on information I had given her. Because my attitude was negative, so was hers. But hers was probably not nearly so opposed as mine. She was also more open-minded about it than I was. When Dr. Stancer had raised the possibility of ECT for me at the beginning of August (this was at the time that he had prescribed Parnate), Beatty phoned Tom Schofield, our psychiatrist friend, and asked for his advice. Reluctant to interfere, Tom had said nothing at first, but Beatty insisted that she really wanted and respected his opinion. His response was short and to the point. "Norm's depression has gone on too long. If ever I were depressed that would be the treatment I would choose." My wife, of course, felt reassured.

After we had both reluctantly agreed to ECT with a great deal of anguish, we went home to lunch. The decision to undergo this treatment was an agonizing one. A few people phoned during the afternoon to ask how I was doing; among them were Irwin and Kathy, two of my closest colleagues and friends. Beatty probably told them about the proposed ECT. About four o'clock that afternoon I received a phone call from Bill, also a psychologist. Because he had been away on sabbatical and had been back in Toronto for only a few weeks, this was the first contact I'd had with him in some time. He said that he was sorry to hear that I had been ill and expressed a desire to visit me to discuss something of the utmost urgency. When asked what it was he wanted to talk about he replied that he had heard that I was contemplating ECT and wanted to warn me against its dangers. He felt that I was too intelligent to subject myself to this treatment. This caused me some agitation and I told him that I didn't want to discuss the matter further because I had already made my decision and that Beatty agreed with me. Bill insisted on coming over that evening. Beatty was worried lest something be said to dissuade me and was not pleased by the proposed visit.

That evening the Dean of Arts joined us and our very good friends the Days, who had just returned from a sabbatical in Israel. The Dean had been to Israel in June to ratify a joint agreement between the Hebrew University in Jerusalem and York University. The conversation, primarily about Israel, was highly enjoyable and I momentarily forgot my troubles. The Dean left about eight-thirty and then Bill arrived.

Bill was pleasant and charming and chatted with the Days about their year abroad. After about a half-hour he and I wandered into the kitchen. He wanted to know why I was willing to "get half my brains burned out" and why I wasn't getting deep psychotherapy. I told him that Beatty and I had thought out our decision very carefully, and further more when one is depressed, one is not readily amenable to psychotherapy. In general, I was so indecisive and so out of it that psychotherapy would have been useless. Psychotherapy is important, but by itself it is no more effective than just waiting for the passage of time to heal such profound depression. Bill said that he knew a psychiatrist who was psychodynamically inclined and who probably wouldn't use ECT. I should get a second opinion. I told Bill no thank you and asked him to leave me alone. Beatty was made very angry by all this.

At 10 o'clock Bill went home, but about an hour later our phone rang. It was Bill. He had phoned his psychiatrist friend who had informed him that he too had used ECT for depression and that it was a safe and effective method. Bill knew that he had upset us and had phoned to apologize. He had meant well and had spoken to us out of genuine concern. He subsequently altered his views on ECT.

One should never interfere when a person is undergoing treatment. Despite his good intentions, Bill should not have tried to undermine Dr. Persad's methods. I hate to admit it, but according to my observations the training in professional and social ethics seems much better for psychiatrists than it is for psychologists. Psychiatrists do not interfere. Yet a number of psychologist colleagues attempted to alter my treatment and were especially concerned about my undergoing ECT without knowing the facts. What are these facts? How is ECT administered? What are the reactions. What effect does it have?

ECT is a relatively simple procedure that can be administered on an outpatient or inpatient basis. In fact, it can be done in the physician's office, with the patient wearing ordinary street clothes. Of course, the shoes are removed. The patient lies on a comfortable bed and is asked to count back from 100. A very fast-acting barbiturate which doubles as an anesthetic is injected intravenously. In my case the anesthetic was sodium pentathol. Within 10 seconds the patient is asleep and remains asleep until after the treatment is completed—usually about 15 to 20 minutes. Immediately after the barbiturate is injected a second chemical, succinylcholine, is injected. It is a relaxant that eliminates all strong muscle contractions and has no serious side effects. In 20 to 30 seconds the muscles relax to a degree that treatment can take place. Both drugs are rapidly metabolized and excreted.

The danger of prolonged apnea (temporary suspension of respiration) after the convulsions is eliminated by giving artificial respiration. This necessitates the presence of an anesthesiologist. The patient can breathe pure oxygen by positive pressure through a face mask which provides full and complete oxygenation of all the body tissues. The patient is then ready for the application of the low-amperage electric current to the temple of the nondominant hemisphere for less than one second. This current is the stimulus that produces the neural discharge and convulsion. Of course, the patient sleeps through it all. The actual treatment takes less than two minutes (not counting the posttreatment sleep of about 20 minutes), and except for the sting of the needle in the first injection (the anesthetic) the patient feels nothing.

Unilateral versus Bilateral ECT. Some temporary confusion and memory loss has occurred in the use of *bilateral ECT,* that is, with electrodes on both temples. This was the standard procedure and is called bilateral ECT because it stimulates both sides of the brain equally. Because of these drawbacks, various modifications have been made. Some practitioners have attempted to use unidirectional currents that involve nonconvulsive electrical stimulation, but because the convulsion seems to be the key factor in the effectiveness of the treatment this method has not gained widespread support. In 1942 Friedman and Wilcox applied electric current to the left side of the head only and produced convulsions. They said nothing about memory loss or confusion nor about how effective this technique was in alleviating depression. In 1949 Goldman used the *unilateral* method, in which one electrode was placed over the nondominant hemisphere, to avoid the speech area. Goldman observed a lessening of confusion and memory loss and noted that the improvement was equal to that of bilateral ECT. In 1956 Thénon used unilateral electroshcok on the nondominant hemisphere and discovered a greatly reduced level of confusion and amnesia.

Lancaster and his colleagues wrote the first English language paper on *unilateral ECT* in which they described the technique of placing electrodes that is now the typical procedure. The lower electrode is applied to the temple in front of the ear and the upper electrode is placed 3 inches higher and at a 70-degree angle to the lower one. Unilateral ECT is less stressful to the person than the bilateral form.

For maximum effectiveness and to minimize confusion and memory loss unilateral ECT should be administered to the nondominant hemisphere or side of the brain. In a right-handed person the right side of the brain is nondominant. In a left-handed person the left side of the brain is nondominant 30 percent of the time and the right side is nondominant 70 percent; that is, 70 percent of the left-handers are like right-handers with respect to brain dominance. The dominant side of the brain contains the speech areas and is believed to be concerned with memory and language functions. It is believed that the nondominant side of the brain is more concerned with emotional and aesthetic functions. Therefore to minimize memory loss and confusion it is desirable that unilateral ECT be administered to the nondominant side of the brain.

Unilateral and bilateral ECT are equally effective in alleviating depression. The advantages of unilateral ECT are that it does not produce post-ECT confusion; it minimizes memory loss and is less stressful to the recipient. A series of 6 to 12 treatments administered on alternate days is usually most effective. Multiple ECT has recently been tried in which several treatments are given in one day, sometimes within a few minutes of one another. This technique is now out of favor.

After the ECT is administered the patient is kept in the recovery room for about 20 minutes until roused from the anesthetic. Initially, there is a groggy feeling but in another 10 minutes or so the patient becomes alert but may have a slight headache. Coffee and cookies are usually served. Outpatients should be accompanied home by a relative or sent home in a taxi; inpatients are returned to their rooms. It is advisable to rest for a few hours. The complete procedure takes less than an hour, but because it is administered under anesthetic the patient feels nothing.

Complications. It is unfortunate that the term "shock" has been used because ECT does not cause shock. The treatment is a safe one and fatalities are extremely rare (about 0.06 percent). Occasionally the patient will suffer a headache and nausea in the recovery phase (I experienced neither one during my course of treatment). Sometimes there is confusion immediately after a treatment (I experienced none). Most patients have mild lapses of memory perhaps after five treatments (I did not), but these losses disappear in a few weeks. Subsequent losses are probably due to remnants of the depression which affects *attention* and not *memory*. Sometimes amenorrhea and weight increase are complications.

What are the after effects of ECT? Does it hurt? In some cases the jaw may ache for a day or two, for if the patient is sensitive to the muscle relaxant this sensitivity will be most pronounced in the strongest muscle of the body, usually the jaw. This can be alleviated with aspirin and rarely occurs after the first treatment. Because muscle relaxants are used, ECT does not cause fractures. Neither does it damage the brain, although it may alter the brain chemistry. As a result the depression is alleviated.

Contraindications. Is it safe to administer ECT to everyone who is depressed? Well, almost everyone. People with brain tumors, extensive brain damage, and other conditions of intracranial pressure should not be given this treatment. ECT should not be administered to anyone who has had a recent myocardial infarction (heart attack) or has a badly damaged heart. If, however, the doctor does not use a barbiturate-type anesthesia, injects succinylcholine as the muscle relaxant, and replaces the barbiturate with a subconvulsive stimulus, the danger to cardiac cases is avoided. There is no danger to patients suffering from hypertension. Peptic ulcers may hemorrhage during ECT and should be taken into account. It is especially important to use muscle relaxant for a patient with a hernia. For cases of glaucoma it should be noted that intraocular pressure decreases during ECT but that succinylcholine increases intraocular pressure. Therefore eserine should be administered to glaucoma patients in advance of ECT. Pregnancy is *not* a contraindication and neither is age. ECT has been administered to persons as old as 87 without complications, but it is probably inadvisable for young people under 16. In effect, brain tumor is basically the only absolute contraindication.

Indications. For whom is ECT indicated? Is it a panacea? ECT is best for severe *bipolar* and *unipolar* affective disorders. Most depressions respond positively to ECT (80 to 100 percent). After three or four treatments the depression starts lifting, and all that is necessary, as a rule, is a course of 6 to 12 treatments. Manic reactions of a bipolar illness can also be treated effectively with ECT, although lithium is to be preferred. It should be noted that affective disorders are recurring illnesses and that lithium has been fairly successful as a prophylactic against manic-depression. The results for reactive and neurotic depressions are not so reliable as they are for bipolar affective (manic-depressive) reactions. ECT has also been used with schizophrenics but not with much success. Psychopharmacological therapy (drug therapy) has largely replaced ECT as the method of treating schizophrenia. ECT has been used in the treatment of psychoneuroses, organic conditions, epilepsy, mental retardation, psychosomatic disorders, acute pain, and personality disorders (e.g., psychopathy), but in general with little success. Perhaps that's why ECT has a bad name—because it has sometimes been used indiscriminately (e.g., *One Flew Over the Cuckoo's Nest*). ECT *is* an effective treatment for depression.

How Does ECT Work?   How and why does ECT work? In 1948 Gordon described "Fifty Shock Therapy Theories." Yet, an acceptable and fully explanatory and convincing theory still needs to be postulated. ECT remains, primarily, an empirical method of treatment with no proved theoretical basis. Most of the psychological theories, such as the punishment hypothesis (e.g., you feel guilty and getting an electric shock is like punishment, after which you feel good) are highly speculative and unconvincing. Some attempts have been made to interpret the effects of ECT on learning and memory. It has been postulated that ECT disrupts the neural consolidation of material that we have already learned and that the cumulative effects of a number of ECT sessions produces a deficit in attention and confusion. The evidence is that there is no permanent memory loss after ECT and that the clinical outcome (alleviation of depression) is independent of changes in memory. Unilateral ECT is as efficacious as bilateral ECT but does not induce significant memory distortion or confusion. The psychological theories really explain nothing, but biological theories have some relevance. Fleming has noted structural changes in the central nervous system, including changes in autonomic functions and cell permeability and endocrine changes. Cronholm and Ottosson, in Sweden, demonstrated that the efficacy of ECT is due primarily to the seizure activity (or more precisely to the cerebral changes that induce the convulsion) and *not* to the intensity of the electrical current. Subconvulsive treatment is *not* beneficial.

   With the advent of the antidepressants in the 1950s and 1960s (e.g., the MAO inhibitors and tricyclics) and their theoretical explanations, for example, the catecholamine hypothesis, similar suggestions have been made for the effectiveness of ECT. It has been suggested that ECT works because it increases the amount of catecholamines in the synaptic junctions of the central nervous system. (As you may recall from Chapter 6, it was suggested that depression is related to a deficit of catecholamines in the central nervous system synapses.)

It appears to be feasible that the intracerebral modifications due to seizure activity are related to increased levels and changes of neurohumors (e.g., catecholamines and serotonin), changes in ionic equilibrium, and increased vascular permeability. The biochemical and biological theories, though incomplete, are more promising as an explanation of ECT than the psychological and psychoanalytic theories. The main thing is that ECT alleviates depression and reduces the frequency of suicide. Dr. Edward Jenner's smallpox vaccine was saving lives before we knew how the antibody-antigen reactions really worked.

The Present Status of ECT. The most recent and comprehensive evaluation of ECT appears in a paper by Albert W. Scovern and Peter R. Kilmann in the March 1980 issue of the *Psychological Bulletin*. The title of their paper is "Status of Electroconvulsive Therapy: Review of the Outcome Literature." Doctors Scovern and Kilmann, who are psychologists, reviewed 60 studies that compared the effectiveness of ECT with that of other methods of treatment or with control procedures. They also examined 30 studies that investigated patient and treatment variables relevant to therapeutic improvement. Despite the methodological deficiencies in many of the studies evaluated, Scovern and Kilman were able to come to a number of conclusions, among which the major premise is that ECT is an effective treatment of endogenous depression, especially when the depression is severe. Because of ECTs fast action, it is particularly warranted when a patient is at the risk for suicide. For endogenous depressives, bipolar or unipolar, ECT is more beneficial than tricyclic antidepressants and particularly more so than MAO inhibitors. ECT does not work well on neurotic or reactive depressions but is most successful with the major affective disorders—unipolar and bipolar endogenous depression.

Serious depression is a recurring illness and there is a high degree of relapse, independent of the type of treatment. The rate of relapse is not higher for an ECT-treated than for a tricyclic drug-treated patient. J.M. Davis, in his summary of the relevent studies, found that 40 to 90 percent of endogenous depressives who were treated with tricyclic antidepressants suffered a relapse when there was no maintenance drug therapy. When there is tricyclic drug prophylaxis, that is, maintenance therapy, the rate of relapse is greatly reduced. Therefore after a course of ECT treatments it is advisable to place patients on a maintenance drug treatment program. For unipolar depressives the tricyclics seem to be most effective and for bipolars lithium by itself or in conjunction with the tricyclics has been useful as a prophylactic against the recurrence of the major affective disorders.

My Course of Treatment.   On Tuesday, August 30, 1977, I agreed to ECT as a course of treatment and was told to return at about 10 o'clock Thursday morning, September 1, for tests and an examination. The ECT would commence on Friday, September 2. On Wednesday morning my good friend Hy Day drove me to York University. I really enjoyed talking to him and I hadn't seen him alone in about six months. He had been in Israel on sabbatical. His company was a great comfort to me. We had lunch together at York, and being at York was not so traumatic this time as it had been the last. After lunch Hy drove me home. When we arrived in my driveway Hy noticed that no one was at home. He offered to go into the house with me, "in case a note had been left for me by Beatty or my daughter." I said that I would be fine and entered the house by myself.

I went upstairs and sure enough there was a note for me. Did Hy know something that I didn't know? The message was to phone Dr. Persad. As I read it I panicked. Why did he want me to phone him? Had he changed his mind about the ECT? Was he now planning to hospitalize me? My secondary depression was really producing para-noid symptoms. I had visions of an ambulance coming to get me to take me to the hospital. And no one was home. Beatty and my daughter were out shopping for groceries. The phone rang. I was afraid to answer. What if it were Dr. Persad phoning me again? The phone stopped ringing. I finally worked up enough courage to call Dr. Persad. The reason he had phoned was a fairly innocuous one. He had wanted me to come for the laboratory tests and examination at nine o'clock instead of at ten because the laboratory closed at nine-thirty. But when one is depressed one always expects the worst. I had made a mountain out of a molehill.

The next morning my wife and I went down to the Clarke Institute for my laboratory tests and examination. I took my sample of urine along. My blood pressure was taken and an EKG (electrocardiogram) and the various blood tests were made. After I had signed the consent form I was given an ECT instruction sheet and asked to report to the sixth floor of the Clarke Institute at seven-forty-five the next morning. The instruction sheet told me to bring slippers, pajamas, and a robe, not to eat or take any medication after midnight, and to arrange for someone to take me home after completion of the procedure. Dr. Persad said that although he was not on duty the next morning to administer the ECT, he would nevertheless meet me on the sixth floor. He knew of my great concern and wanted to reassure me. He explained all the details to me, but I was still worried. (I tried to diminish my anxiety by jokingly referring to ECT as getting ''zapped.'' My wife didn't think that was funny.)

The next morning, Friday, I awoke bright and early and started bugging Beatty about getting to the Clarke Institute on time. Although it normally takes about 40 minutes to get there (and should take even less time at the crack of dawn when there is little traffic), I felt that we should leave ourselves at least an hour. I was really worried. Beatty humored me and we left home a few minutes before seven and arrived at the Clarke Institute shortly after seven-thirty. Dr. Persad met us on the sixth floor at seven-forty-five. He tried to calm me down, and I recall his saying that he had never seen anyone so agitated as I. The prospect of ECT really frightened me.

Beatty remained in the waiting area and Dr. Persad and I went into the ECT room. I changed into my pajamas and a nurse took my vital signs (blood pressure, pulse, and temperature). The nurse and other attendants were friendly and reassuring. I began to feel at ease. The anesthetist arrived and informed me that she was going to give me an injection. I was asked to lie down on a cot and was wheeled into the ECT room proper. It was about eight o'clock. A needle was injected into my arm and I was told to count back from 100. I got about as far as 91. The next thing I knew I was in the recovery room and it was about eight-fifteen. I was slightly groggy and tired but not confused. My memory was not impaired. I certainly knew where I was. I rested for another few minutes and was then given some cookies and coffee. Shortly after eight-thirty, I got dressed, went down the hall to fetch Beatty, and she drove me home. At home I had breakfast and then lay down for a few hours. Late in the morning I got dressed. I felt no pain, no confusion, and no agitation. I felt neither less depressed nor more depressed than I had before the ECT.

Although I was not agitated, I was tense, but this had nothing to do with the ECT. This was the Labor Day weekend and we were expecting visitors from Ottawa—my wife's sister, my brother-in-law, their three children, and their dog. I didn't think that I could handle all these visitors. I had enough to worry about without visitors. In all fairness Beatty had consulted me about inviting them, and because I felt that she wanted and needed company I had agreed. Nevertheless, I was still worried. My concern was needless. My brother-in-law and sister-in-law were most sympathetic and understanding and despite my misgivings the visit was not too onerous. We went downtown on Saturday (where I was concerned about getting lost) and to the Toronto zoo on Sunday. They left on Monday. That evening Beatty and I went out to dinner with some friends. In general, the weekend went fairly well, although I was concerned about my next ECT, which was scheduled for Tuesday.

Normally the ECT is administered on Mondays, Wednesdays, and Fridays, but because of the holiday, the treatments were scheduled that week for Tuesday, Wednesday, and Friday (September 6, 7, and 9). After about the third or fourth treatment I began to feel somewhat better. I started perking up. After the third treatment I went up to Dr. Persad's office and spoke to him briefly. He asked me if I had noticed any improvement and to what degree. I believed that I had improved 35 to 40 percent. Dr. Persad believed that the improvement was more likely to be 70 to 75 percent. My fifth and sixth treatments were on Monday, September 12, and Wednesday, September 14. I felt fine after my sixth treatment, but Dr. Persad suggested that I come back for an extra one (a seventh one) on Friday, September 16. This made sense to me. We were planning to go to Montreal on Saturday, September 17, for the weekend, for my nephew's Bar Mitzvah. It was essential that I be in good shape because my mother did not know then (nor does she know now) about my depression.

On Thursday, September 15, my daughter's sixteenth birthday, Hy Day drove me into the office in the morning. I went into the chairman's office merely intending to stay for an hour or so. Kathy was there and I asked her to remain. She stated that she would be glad to stay as long as I needed her assistance. By early afternoon Kathy looked at me and said

"Norm, you are perfectly fine, you do not need me here." She left and I stayed the rest of the day. As of then I resumed the chairmanship full time. A miracle had happened in two weeks. I had gone from feeling like an emotional cripple to feeling well. In a sense, I was on top of the world. Perhaps I was feeling too well. Perhaps there was "a little night music" in me.

My last ECT session was the next morning, and that evening my wife and I went to a symphony concert and on Saturday to Montreal for the weekend. On the next Wednesday, September 21, I taught my first class; I also played my first game of tennis in more than three months and won. That night my sex drive returned. September 21—my holiday of darkness was over and fall arrived with a bang!

Postscript. Negative attitudes about ECT die hard. A few months later, in November, my wife and I went to New York with some friends for the weekend. I phoned another friend who is a professor of psychology and a clinician at a well-known eastern university. He has also written a textbook (which has gone through a few editions) on personality. I arranged to meet him, briefly, in New York. When we met I told him about my depression and about ECT. His response was "Oh, my gosh! How could you let them do this to you, Norm." I smiled to myself!

8

A Little Night Music

It was great to be alive again. It was inconceivable that I had recovered so rapidly and so well. One day I was down in the dumps, destined to be an emotional cripple for the rest of my life; the next I was back to my normal self, as if nothing had happened. At times I felt as if I were on top of the world. Graham Reed, the Dean of the Faculty of Graduate Studies, was right. He had told me that the day the depression lifted everything would be back to normal and I would be functioning as I always had. But I hadn't believed him. In fact, I swore at him. The next time I saw him I apologized to him for being a "doubting Thomas."

Mid-September was the beginning of the academic school year and I quickly took charge of things. I chaired the executive committee and departmental meetings; I started making arrangements for recruiting new faculty and for the Promotions and Tenure Committee to function. I reactivated the Departmental Committee on Goals and Objectives. I met with my research assistants and discussed my research project on anxiety. I arranged to meet my classes. When I was concerned that I might not return to work by September, I had made tentative plans for my coteacher of the graduate seminar on social influence processes to teach the first term. Now that I was feeling well, I agreed to do so. My coteacher was relieved because he had a heavy teaching and administrative load for the first term.

I resumed my regular tennis program and my regular social life. My sex life was better than ever before. I ate and slept regularly. I felt neither tense nor anxious. In fact, I felt good. But most of all I talked. Gee whiz, did I ever talk. I talked from morning until night. I talked incessantly. I talked nonstop and then more so. I told everyone about my illness, my treatment, and my recovery. I referred to the ECT by telling everyone how I had had my brain "zapped." My explanation for talking so much was twofold. One, I was so pleased to be alive and well that I wanted to share my experience with everyone. Two, I felt that being a little high was a rebound from the depression and caused by the ECT. I did not realize it at the time but I was probably hypomanic.

During September and October I was seeing Dr. Persad about once a week, or once every 10 days, primarily to make sure that everything was OK with me. About the beginning of October I was taken off medication completely. I had been taking some nortriptyline (Aventyl), some Valium, and some sleeping pills, but because I hated taking drugs Dr. Persad agreed that I could drop them. He was concerned, however, about my hypomanic behavior and raised the possibility of giving me lithium if things didn't quiet down in a few months. Beatty was also upset by my hypomanic behavior, especially my incessant talking. In fact, she phoned Dr. Persad about it one day and he asked her to tell me to phone him. I was furious with Beatty for phoning Dr. Persad "behind my back." I accused her of resenting my recovery and was highly argumentative and hostile toward her. Yet I accused her of being hostile toward me. All this is part of the hypomanic pattern of behavior. I was hypomanic during September, October, and the first part of November.

All that fall I had no realization of hypomania. After Beatty spoke to Dr. Persad I went down to the Clarke Institute to see him. I told Dr. Persad that I was a person of high energy and that because he did not know anything about my premorbid (preillness) personality he couldn't really tell whether I was hypomanic or whether this was basically my ordinary operating level. Beatty felt that my behavior was qualitatively different from what it had been before I became ill. I discounted her opinion and told her again that she resented my being well. My reasoning was that during my depression I had been almost totally dependent on her and that she felt really needed. Now that I was well I could do things on my own. I believed she resented it and tried to cramp my style. Although it is true that she had been under a tremendous strain all summer and was merely letting up now, unconsciously she may have been somewhat upset by my rapid recovery. In retrospect I now realize that I was hypomanic during that period and that she was genuinely concerned about my health. Furthermore, she probably dreaded another ordeal like that summer. Although my children were annoyed by my constant chatter, they were not so concerned about my general behavior as my wife was. At times, I was hostile and irritable with them as well as with my wife, and at times my behavior toward some of my colleagues was equally hostile.

I was not really fully aware of my behavior nor of the effect that it had on others. During my depression I was quite introspective. As a hypomanic, however, I didn't stop to analyze my thoughts, feelings, or behavior. I was much too busy and didn't always stop to think about what I was doing. Therefore much of what follows about my hypomanic behavior is based on what others subsequently told me rather than on self-analysis. I was critical of others and occasionally told some people off publicly. I was not so concerned about others as I had been nor of the effect my behavior had on them. I was aggressive, talked incessantly, and interrupted others while they were speaking. Whenever I had a thought I felt compelled to utter it, and I didn't always censor my thoughts and feelings. At times I seemed to have lost my sense of judgment. This was quite different from my usual pattern of behavior, but I was not aware of the discrepancy. Except for my wife (and Dr. Persad), no one else told me that my behavior was qualitatively different from what it had been. I was having a good time, I was narcissistically preoccupied with myself, but (without being aware of it) I was making my wife miserable.

Although my behavior may have been hypomanic, it was not basically pathological. I did nothing indiscreet. By the first or second week in November I was back to a normal level and Dr. Persad dropped the idea of my taking lithium. During the first week in November Beatty and I and some friends went to New York for a weekend and I believe that I was perfectly normal then. In mid-November I went to southern California for a conference and on the way there stopped over at Stanford University. At Stanford I stayed with Marilyn (my research assistant) and her husband and made arrangements to spend my next sabbatical (1979/1980) at the university (this book was written at Stanford in 1979/1980).

The conference was on organizational development, and I stayed with Bill, who was on sabbatical in southern California. This is the same Bill who three months before (in August) had advised me against having ECT. In fact, while I was staying at his house we discussed the whole issue. He apologized for interfering and admitted that he should have got the facts before saying anything. His heart was in the right place. He was genuinely concerned about my well being and was trying to help me. He also recognized that one should not interfere in an ongoing case in which one is not the therapist. Both Bill and his wife were excellent hosts and I had a marvellous time. It was about this time that I came down from my high and back to a more normal mood.

Late in September or early October Dr. Persad asked me if I had ever thought about writing about my depression. He felt that by combining my experiences as a clinical psychologist with my experiences as a patient I might have an important contribution to make. I hadn't thought about it, but after some reflection I agreed that it seemed like a good idea. A number of books about depression have been published; some by former patients and some by professionals. To the best of my knowledge there had never been a book about depression by a professional who was also a former patient. I told Dr. Persad that I had no reservations about using my own name, but he told me to think about it carefully. I discussed this matter with my wife and she saw nothing wrong with it. Dr. Persad said that if I felt comfortable about using my own name he foresaw no difficulty.

When I told Dr. Stancer (the consultant on affective disorders at the Clarke Institute) about my plan he was strongly opposed to the idea initially. Although he himself saw no stigma attached to mental illness, he felt that society as a whole did and that it could ruin my career. On further reflection he felt that perhaps the use of my own name might not be harmful. I then asked my good friend Tom Schofield for his opinion. He thought that there would be nothing wrong in my using my own name. He also noted, and I agreed with him, that psychiatrists have made a considerable contribution to the stigma that is attached to mental illness. If psychiatrists cannot have the same attitude toward depression that they have toward appendicitis, how can they expect the lay public to maintain a benign attitude toward depression! Surely, if I had wanted to write a book about my gall bladder operation no one would have questioned my judgment in using my own name. Surely, no one would have suggested sending me out of town for that operation in 1961. Yet in 1977 it was suggested that if I needed hospitalization for my depression I should leave Toronto.

I had planned to start writing my book on depression in the fall of 1977, but in my hypomanic state I planned many things. Fortunately, I did not start writing it until the fall of 1979 while on sabbatical at Stanford University. I say fortunately because the intervening two years had provided me with some perspective and a more realistic view of my depression and of myself in general.

Dr. Persad had first diagnosed my illness as a unipolar depression, but after observing my hypomanic behavior, my "little night music," in the fall of 1977 he revised his diagnosis and classified my illness as a bipolar affective disorder (i.e., a manic-depressive disorder). The chances of recurrence of a bipolar disorder are fairly high. Yet because I had not had a recurrence Dr. Persad agreed to wait before prescribing lithium as a prophylactic.

During mid-December of that year Beatty and I went to Cancun, Mexico. My wife was extremely reluctant to go because she hates hot and humid weather. She went for my sake, however, but resolved never to go again. I had a wonderful time swimming, playing tennis, enjoying the sun, and visiting the pyramids built by the Maya Indians. Beatty hated it. She claimed that I had made the arrangements in late October or early November without consulting her and that this was another manifestation of my hypomanic behavior. I claimed that because I hadn't had a vacation the summer before I needed the sun and rest. No doubt we were both right. I may have been hypomanic when I planned the trip, but I believe I was normal during the trip. The "little night music" was over.

January, February, March, and the first half of April 1978 were uneventful. During January of 1978 I received a Canadian Silver Jubilee Medal from the Governor General of Canada to commemorate the twenty-fifth anniversary of the accession of Queen Elizabeth II (1952–1977) to the British throne. This was a complete surprise to me and I was pleased and gratified. I later found out that the President of York University had nominated me for this award. It was completely unexpected but totally appreciated. In February I received a phone call from the Director of the Institute of Behavioral Research at Texas Christian University (TCU) in Fort Worth, who informed me that they were planning to invite a number of distinguished visitors to come to TCU in the next few months to discuss issues in personality theory, especially those related to persons versus situations, and the role of person by situation interactions in behavior. I was asked to participate because they considered me one of the leading experts in the field. I readily agreed to go for a few days during the middle of April and to lecture on April 13. That would give me sufficient time to prepare the lecture and to get ready for my visit to Oxford University in May and June of 1978.

In May 1977 I was informed that I had been awarded a Travel Fellowship by the British Council (only members of the British Commonwealth are eligible). The Department of Experimental Psychology at Oxford University in conjunction with a number of other British Universities had nominated me for this award, which became effective April 1, 1978, and which was for Distinguished University Scholars. I was planning to go for about six weeks in May and June 1978. My home base would be Oxford, but I would also visit a number of other universities including Sheffield, Sussex, and the London School of Economics. The terms of reference were flexible. I would be giving a number of lectures, I would talk primarily to graduate students and faculty, and I would do my own writing and scholarly work. My sponsor was Dr. Michael Argyle, probably one of the leading social psychologists in Europe. I was looking forward eagerly to this trip. Kathy had agreed to serve as acting chairman while I was away.

The last time I saw Dr. Persad was in January. I was not supposed to see him again until the end of April which was just before my trip to Oxford. Sometime during March Dr. Persad informed me that the Clarke Institute was having a series of panel discussions on various mental health issues and that one of them would be on depression. They were planning to show a short video tape on depression and he asked if I would be willing to be interviewed by him and video taped anonymously. This tape would be viewed solely on the evening of Tuesday, April 11, and would not be shown subsequently without my permission. I readily agreed to the interview and at the end of March went down to the Clarke Institute for the taping. It was nice seeing Dr. Persad again. The interview was spontaneous and unrehearsed and the taping went well. About 10 to 12 minutes were filmed. Dr. Persad invited Beatty and me to a small dinner party at the Clarke Institute on Tuesday, April 11, to be held before the panel discussion on depression. (I was to leave for TCU on Wednesday, April 12.) The dinner party was also to be attended by Dr. Persad and his wife, Dr. Stancer and his wife, Dr. Lowy, former Chief of the Clarke Institute of Psychiatry and currently Dean of Medicine, University of Toronto, and his wife, and June Callwood, a writer and radio and television star. The panel participants were to be Drs. Persad, Lowy, and Stancer (Dr. Lowy had the flu on

April 11 and was unable to participate), with June Callwood serving as moderator.

We met in Dr. Persad's office and then went to the eighth floor of the Clarke for dinner. It was a pleasant and relaxing event. After dinner we all went down to the auditorium and Beatty and I sat in the audience. The panel discussion was most interesting and Beatty thought that I had handled myself well during the interview. I had no reaction one way or another to seeing and hearing myself talk about my depression. I was not concerned about being recognized, but I was quieter than usual.

Both Beatty and I related my attitude to a gum infection. I had been to the dentist the week before to have my teeth cleaned. On Friday an irritation began in my gums which continued on Saturday, so much so that I had difficulty concentrating on my tennis game. Saturday morning, after tennis, I went over to the emergency ward of the North York General Hospital. (My dentist's office was closed on Saturday.) The duty doctor prescribed some penicillin and told me to see my dentist on Monday. I felt very tired, but I took the penicillin and either rested in bed or slept most of the weekend. Neither my wife nor I found this unusual and assumed that my behavior was due to my dental problem.

On Monday I returned to work and everything seemed fine. Monday afternoon I went to the dentist; he cleaned up the infection and told me to finish taking the penicillin. On Tuesday I consulted during the day at the Department of Psychiatry, Toronto East General Hospital, and that evening Beatty and I went to the Clarke Institute of Psychiatry for the panel discussion on depression. On Wednesday I was to leave for Texas Christian University. I wakened very early Wednesday morning and recall that Beatty remarked that I didn't seem particularly enthusiastic about my trip and that I had been unusually quiet at dinner the night before. My wife drove me to the limousine and I left for the airport. I felt somewhat anxious and realized that I didn't really want to make this trip. The only other thing that had seemed untoward during the week was that my sex drive seemed to be diminishing.

When I arrived at the Fort Worth-Dallas Airport one of the graduate students drove me to my motel in Fort Worth. I felt tense and listless, and at lunch I didn't feel like eating. After lunch I went to my room for an hour before being met by a faculty member who was to give me a tour of Fort Worth. While waiting I lay down on my bed and rested.

Although I was very tired, I couldn't fall asleep. My throat was dry. I was jumpy and jittery and felt a lump in my throat. I was nervous. In short, I was beginning to feel depressed. However, by the time the faculty member arrived to give me a tour of the city I felt fine. The afternoon was uneventful and it was good to be outdoors in the Texas sunshine. A number of us went out for dinner and drinks and I got back to the motel shortly after 10 o'clock. I went to bed early but couldn't sleep. Anxiety gripped me and I kept worrying about the possibility of having to cancel my trip to Oxford. What was I to do? I was panic-stricken. Would I be able to present my lecture the following evening? Finally, after much tossing and turning I fell asleep. When I awoke I was still tense. Except for my penicillin, I had no medication with me. I had no tranquilizers to calm my frayed nerves.

On Thursday I was given a tour of the facilities of the Institute of Behavioral Research and met the director. About 10 o'clock I became anxious, tense, and restless. My throat was dry and I still had the lump. After about an hour my anxiety disappeared. At noon I played tennis with one of the faculty members and had a most enjoyable time. It was great being outdoors and playing tennis. During the afternoon I met a number of the researchers and we discussed our mutual research interests. I had difficulty focusing on the topic. The director of the Institute and his wife took me to the country club for dinner and we had an excellent meal. After dinner I presented my lecture and all went well. I was not at all nervous during my talk. After the lecture there was a party in my honor and I was then taken back to my motel. Again, I had difficulty falling asleep and this made me nervous and tense. I was extremely worried that my depression was returning.

On Friday another faculty member was to give me a tour of the art galleries and museums, and then I was to play tennis, have lunch, and attend a graduate seminar in psychology. During the tour of the art galleries my anxiety mounted and I was also feeling low, but when the time came to play tennis I perked up. The graduate seminar went well, and a number of us went to a very fancy restaurant for dinner. A few of us then went on for drinks. I had a wonderful time and forgot all about my troubles. I arrived at my motel shortly after midnight and again had difficulty falling asleep. I kept tossing and turning. What was to become of me? I didn't really know. I was scheduled to leave for Toronto Saturday afternoon.

Saturday morning a faculty member, his wife and their baby, and I went to the zoo. Although it was a lovely zoo, I became impatient and irritable. I couldn't stand still for a moment. I was tense and nervous and had butterflies in my stomach. After lunch a graduate student took me to the airport, where we had a drink before I left. I was beginning to feel the fog closing in again. They served food on the plane but I couldn't eat it. I rationalized this by saying that it was just as well because my wife and I had been invited out for dinner in Toronto that night. When I arrived home, my wife asked me how I felt. I said that I thought that I would be OK, but because of my tenseness I was planning to phone Dr. Persad on Monday morning. I took a tranquilizer (Valium) and we went off to the dinner party where we had a Danish meal with aquavit, herring, and the rest. It was just lovely. On Sunday Beatty and I went to an art gallery and then over to have coffee with Morris and his wife. Although I took a few tranquilizers during the day, I was still nervous and tense.

9
Here We Go Again!

On the Monday morning after my trip to Forth Worth and TCU I phoned Dr. Persad. Dr. Persad saw me that afternoon at five and I told him what had happened. He prescribed Elavil, told me to phone him in a few days, and to see him again on Friday (the Friday appointment had been scheduled, routinely, in January). He assured me that because Elavil was the purest form of amitriptyline I would not experience the urinary retention that I had had with Deprex and Levate. Elavil, Levate, and Deprex are different trade names for amitriptyline, one of the tricyclics. The only thing that differentiates them is their binding. I honestly don't believe that differences in binding would produce differential side effects. I think that Dr. Persad was using "psychology" on me. But it worked. Although I did have some difficulty in urinating with Elavil, the side effects were not so serious as they had been with Levate and Deprex. Furthermore, this time I avoided the hysteria that had accompanied the urinary tetention. Dr. Persad told me to start off with 25 mg a day and work my way up to 75 mg. He also told me to take a daily dose of 10 to 15 mg of Valium.

On Wednesday afternoon I went to the stadium with Kathy to see the Blue Jays play the Yankees. I asked her if she would drive. I didn't feel up to it, but didn't tell her so! It was a good game, but I had difficulty concentrating. Fortunately Kathy had to leave before the game was over because she was going to the opera that night. She drove me home about six-thirty. Nobody was home and I reacted with fright. Beatty and my daughter soon came home. They had been out shopping. My son was still at the baseball game. I was really feeling low, listless, and tense.

Thursday morning I phoned Dr. Persad and told him that I was still depressed. He suggested that I come in to see him at eight-thirty on Friday instead of at noon, as previously scheduled. As I guessed (correctly), he was planning on ECT as a course of treatment and wanted to take some tests beforehand. Because he wanted to get me ready for Oxford at the beginning of May (it was already April 21), he believed that ECT would be the quickest and most efficient form of treatment. My son was going down to the university on Friday morning so he drove down with me. At first I suggested that he drive but he told me to go ahead. Although I was tense I had no difficulty making it to the Clarke Institute. My son was to meet me at noon and we were to go to York University in the afternoon. Dr. Persad informed me he was planning a series of ECT treatments beginning on Monday, April 24, and took various tests which included an EKG, pulse rate, and blood pressure. He also arranged for me to have a blood test. I readily agreed to the ECT because it had been so dramatically effective the last time. He did not know how many treatments would be needed.

The first Passover Seder was that Friday night, April 21. My mother had arrived the night before by train from Montreal for the Passover holiday. She had not been told about my first depression the year before nor did we want her to know about this one. It would have been impossible to be with her had she known. My mother's visit plus my depression placed an extra strain on all of us, especially my wife, who would have to deal with it all to a greater extent than the rest of us. We did manage, however, to hide the fact of my depression from my mother.

After I saw Dr. Persad I went to a case conference at the Clarke Institute, where I was still a consultant. I could not concentrate on what was going on because I was too preoccupied with myself and with my depression. I was partly in a fog. After the case conference Harvey, Morris, and I went to a Chinese (Szechuan) restaurant for lunch. We were met there by my son. After lunch my son and I went to York University. He drove. I met with one of my research assistants about my research on anxiety, and she showed me some data, but I couldn't focus on the task. After that I saw Kathy and explained to her that my depression had returned. I asked her if she could chair the department executive and departmental general meetings scheduled for Monday, April 24. Kathy was supposed to serve as acting chairman while I was at Oxford, beginning May 1. I asked her if she could take over a week earlier and she readily agreed. She said that she had noticed that I was unusually quiet and unsure of myself at the baseball game and was thinking of commenting on it, but hadn't. She told me not to worry because she would look after things. On Monday morning she would tell the department that I had to go to the dentist. It was reassuring to have Kathy in charge.

Friday night I conducted the first Passover Seder. Although I was very quiet and passive, it went very smoothly. The Seder was attended by my wife, son, daughter, and mother. For the Second Seder, also given at our house, my cousins and their families joined us. Although it was a strain for me to have all the extra people in the house, there was no trouble. It was surprising that nobody noticed my depression. There are probably thousands of depressed people in North America whom nobody notices. Yet if someone engages in acting out behavior everyone notices. Except for being quieter than usual, my overt behavior was no different from the normal. Inside I was seething with tension and anguish. With much effort I got through the weekend. I was too nervous to drive the car. When we went out my daughter drove and we explained this to my mother by saying she wanted to practice her driving. Bright and early Monday morning my son took me to the Clarke Institute for my first ECT. We arrived at the Clarke Institute at seven-forty-five. This time I was not anxious about the ECT. I was resigned to the fact that it was both necessary and beneficial. Unlike the time before, I no longer had a negative attitude. This time I did not joke about it. I did not talk about getting my brain "zapped." I took it quite seriously and now had achieved a very positive attitude.

Because my wife and I were supposed to go to Oxford in 10 days, Dr. Persad had planned a concentrated series of ECT sessions. For a start I was to have five sessions in five days during the week of April 24. After the first session on Monday I woke up feeling disoriented, but I recognized immediately where I was. I went home, rested for the remainder of the morning, and was then driven into York by my son. I was able to interact with others, despite my anxiety and depression, but I did have difficulty concentrating on my work. I was certainly not in the shape as I had been early the summer before. Monday night I was pleased to see Hy. He also came to say goodbye to my mother who was returning to Montreal the next morning. I stayed home Tuesday and Wednesday after the treatments, and Thursday afternoon I went to work. Friday I stayed home after the treatment. After five treatments I still hadn't noticed any improvement and was positive that I wouldn't be able to go to Oxford. I was prepared to cancel the trip. Dr. Persad and Beatty both thought I had made some improvement, albeit not so dramatic as that of the previous September. Dr. Persad persuaded me to delay making a decision about the Oxford trip. We had been scheduled to leave about May 3.

Dr. Persad scheduled some additional ECT treatments for the following week. After the treatment on Monday, May 1, Beatty phoned Michael Argyle at Oxford to inform him that I was depressed and that our trip to England was going to be delayed. (It was difficult tracking him down because May 1 was a holiday in England.) My wife told him she would call him again when our plans were more definite. Michael was sympathetic and understanding, but my first lecture was not scheduled until Monday, May 15, at Sheffield University. Therefore the delay was not serious.

My seventh ECT treatment was on Tuesday, May 2. What a way to celebrate my forty-seventh birthday. Birthday celebrations were the furthest things from my mind, however. I was becoming disturbed that after seven treatments I was still feeling depressed. In September my depression had lifted completely after seven treatments. Why the difference? It is impossible to say for sure, but a number of possibilities present themselves. The time before I did not have the ECT sessions until after I had been depressed for more than three months. Now I was having the treatments at the beginning of my depression. Even though the medication had produced no dramatic results the year before, it must have had some effect over a period of three months. During the course of a depression changes take place despite the treatment. It is possible that the earlier depression was just beginning to lift and the ECT facilitated this healing process. It is possible also that concentrated ECT (every day) does not work so well as distributed ECT (every few days). Finally, no two depressions are exactly the same even in the same person.

My eighth treatment was on Wednesday, there was no treatment on Thursday, and my ninth was on Friday, May 5. Dr. Persad scheduled a tenth for Monday, May 8. We celebrated my wife's birthday on Sunday, May 7. It probably wasn't much of a celebration for her, but she knew and I knew that I would be getting better soon. After my ECT session on Monday Dr. Persad told me to see him again on Tuesday afternoon so that we might reevaluate my progress and decide on my trip to Oxford. He seemed to think that I was improving but I felt as if I were at a standstill. I went to the University on Monday afternoon. I was still unable to drive so my wife took me in. Again, I was able to chat with my colleagues but had difficulty in concentrating on any work. However, I was able to function effectively in my interpersonal relationships.

Early Tuesday afternoon my wife and I went downtown. I believe that we had lunch and then wandered around before seeing Dr. Persad in the late afternoon. After talking to Dr. Persad for a few minutes he suggested an eleventh ECT session for the first thing Wednesday morning, May 10. There would be time to make a final decision by early Wednesday afternoon. He implied that he felt that I could go and that he would give me a letter of introduction to a psychiatrist in Oxford in the event I needed to see one. In any case, the final decision would have to be mine. Beatty, too, felt that it would be appropriate to go and that I could handle it. She felt that I had made some improvement during the last few weeks.

On Wednesday morning I had my eleventh ECT session and then went home and rested. After much thought I reluctantly decided to go. My decision was based more on a sense of commitment than on feeling up to it. I phoned Dr. Persad and informed him of my decision. He sounded pleased. Beatty arranged to get new plane tickets (she had cancelled the old ones) and sent Michael Argyle a night letter to tell him we were coming.

Our plan was to leave Toronto on Thursday, May 11 (arriving in London on Friday, May 12), and to stay in England for four weeks. I spent most of Thursday organizing my notes for my lectures at Oxford and other British universities. To my surprise I was able to produce some outlines and to decide which reprints and articles to take. Although it took me longer than usual, I believe I did an effective job. Evidently, when the pressure was on I was able to manage. This gave me some much needed confidence. While I was preparing for my talks my wife picked up the plane tickets, went to the bank, and packed our clothes. The way she arranged things was fantastic—and without losing her cool.

Our son drove us to the airport that evening and we left about eight o'clock. I was exhausted, tense, and anxious. I attempted to urinate before our plane left but was unable to do so. I guess it was more

difficult to urinate in a public washroom. I tried again on the plane
without success. I had difficulty falling asleep, probably because I was
apprehensive about the trip in general and more specifically because of
the recurring urinary retention. We arrived at London's Heathrow
Airport at about seven-thirty Friday morning, I asleep on my feet. My
exhaustion was due both to my depression and the flight. We took the
bus to Reading and the train to Oxford. At the Oxford station we took a
taxi to Halifax House where we were staying, next door to the
psychology department. We registered and made our way to our room
which was on the third floor. I staggered into the bathroom, which was
down the hall. After some hesitation I urinated. At last! I guess when
one is very tired and one has to go, one goes—depression or no
depression. What a relief, both physically and psychologically.

My wife and I were hungry and tired. We slept until late afternoon. I
then went over to the Psychology Department and tried to find Michael.
He was out of town. I tried to reach Sheffield University to confirm my
talk on Monday, but without success. C'est la vie! My wife and I took a
walk into town and then came back to Halifax House for dinner. Halifax
House is a residence for graduate students and visiting scholars. It is
quaint and austere, but the rooms are of ample size. There is a basin and
heater in each one but no toilet, tub, or shower, not a very cheerful
place to stay when one is depressed. Some might say that it is not a
cheerful place even when one is not depressed. No meals are served
from Saturday after lunch until Monday morning. On Sundays a kettle
and tea are provided for each room. At the most the accommodations
were adequate and convenient.

On Saturday morning we received a phone call from my cousin and
her husband. They were visiting England from Toronto and were
staying overnight at Oxford. We asked them to come over to our place
and planned to spend the day with them. A few minutes later Michael
Argyle knocked on our door. He had been out of town and had returned
late Friday night. We were delighted to see him. We spoke to him for a
while and he invited us to his home on Sunday afternoon for high tea. A
few minutes after Michael left, my cousin and her husband arrived and
we walked into the downtown area of Oxford and toward the book-
stores.

For my stay at Oxford Dr. Persad had supplied me with maintenance
dosages of Elavil and Valium. I was to take 75 mg of Elavil (25 mg,
three times a day) and 20 mg of Valium (5 mg four times a day). A

small amount of Elavil probably wouldn't do too much for my depression, but it would enable Dr. Persad to raise it to a more therapeutic dose when I returned to Toronto. The Valium was meant to alleviate or at least diminish my anxiety. Dr. Persad did not want to give me too much medication without the proper day-to-day medical supervision. I had been taking this level of medicine (Elavil and Valium) since the time of my first ECT session in April. According to my perception, it did not seem to affect me one way or the other. Dr. Persad said that I would have been worse without the medication. He felt that it was essential that I continue taking it and because I had faith in him I did so.

Just before noon I suddenly became dizzy, broke into a sweat, and generally felt extremely groggy. We all went back to the room and I took a Valium. We then went to a pub for lunch and I felt better. I guess it was a combination of anxiety, fatigue, and hunger. During the afternoon we explored the stores and colleges of Oxford, stopped for high tea, and then did some more walking. It was an enjoyable afternoon. We then looked around for a place for dinner and found a lovely French restaurant. During dinner I felt very hot and again broke into a sweat. I had difficulty in concentrating and felt dazed and claustrophobic. I had to get out of the restaurant. We all left before coffee and went for a walk. The fresh air made me feel better. I guess I was really exhausted. My wife and I said goodbye to our cousins and went back to our room. It had been great seeing them and on balance I guess I had a nice day. We put on the heater in our room and covered ourselves with blankets to hold off the cold. This was the middle of May, but Oxford didn't know that. I must have been really tired because I slept until eleven the next morning.

My wife and I made ourselves some tea which we had with crackers, cheese, and jam. This was our breakfast. I finally reached Sheffield and my wife and I walked down to the train station to buy our tickets for the next day. We then had a snack and returned to our room. Michael picked us up about three-thirty and we went to his house for tea. His wife, Sonia, was very warm and friendly and we had a very nice time. Beatty and I then went home and rested and then out for dinner at another French restaurant. This time I enjoyed my meal and nothing unusual happened. We went to bed early because we were leaving for Sheffield the next morning.

Michael met us at the station the next morning because he was going to Northern England and taking the same train to Birmingham. We changed trains at Birmingham and arrived about one-thirty at Sheffield, where we were met by one of the psychologists. We had tea and he showed us the center for the performing arts in Sheffield. My wife went back to the hotel and I went to the university to give my talk. I had no trouble with my presentation and we had a lively discussion. I then went back to the hotel to rest. At six-thirty our host came to get us and we toured the Pennines before having dinner. The next day I visited the psychology laboratories at the University of Sheffield and I then attended another seminar. We returned to Oxford late Tuesday afternoon.

On Friday, May 19, my wife and I took the train to Brighton where I gave a lecture at the University of Sussex. Brighton is the beach area, south of London, and was King Edward VII's playground when he was Prince of Wales. There are nice alleys for shopping and the Royal Pavilion, a palace of Moorish-Chinese-Indian architecture. My talk, which was on Friday afternoon, went quite well and my wife and I and a few of the psychologists went to a lovely French restaurant for dinner. Because Brighton is such a beautiful area, we decided to stay over until Sunday morning. Although I was still depressed and occasionally anxious and agitated, I found it enjoyable to walk on the boardwalk in the sun. The interesting thing is that although both my wife and I knew that I was depressed none of the psychologists at the University of Sussex picked it up. Because we had not met before, they probably assumed that I was quiet, shy, introverted, and reticent. Perhaps it's easier to "pass" for OK when you are depressed than for any other emotional problem.

On Sunday morning we left Brighton and stopped off in London on the way back to Oxford. We visited the British Museum and walked some of the streets of London. For some undiscernible reason I was anxious. Perhaps I was afraid of getting lost. Perhaps the tension of having to "perform" at the University of Sussex was getting to me. Nevertheless, I did enjoy visiting the British Museum and I did enjoy riding the Underground, despite my fear of disorientation. Before returning to Oxford we obtained information on various hotels near the British Museum. I was scheduled to present a talk at the London School of Economics at the end of May and my wife and I were planning to spend a few days in London.

On Tuesday, May 23, I presented a colloquium on "The Interactional Model of Anxiety" at Oxford. The talk was well received, although I had been quite worried about giving it. This is atypical of me because I have never minded speaking before any group. But a depression does strange things. Perhaps I felt inadequate, but in retrospect I guess that giving a talk at Oxford is like giving a talk anywhere else. There was really nothing to intimidate me, for I was scheduled to give a second colloquim on "Personality Models" on Tuesday, June 6.

The day after my first Oxford colloquium, which was Wednesday, May 24, the Argyles and my wife and I went down to the Cherwell river, not too far from where it joins the Thames, to watch the "Eights Races." This was "Eights Week," when all the colleges at Oxford have their boat races. Each boat contains eight rowers, hence the name "Eights Week." It was exciting to watch the races and as part of the festivities we had the traditional strawberries and cream. Beatty and I returned on Saturday for the finals and joined a contingent of Canadian graduate students and visiting Canadian faculty. We picnicked along the river on wine and cheese and crackers and of course had strawberries and cream again. It was a glorious sunny Saturday afternoon and I almost forgot my depression. But not quite. I still felt as if there were a barrier between the others and me.

The next morning, Sunday, May 28, my wife and I took the train to London. Beatty had arranged for us to stay at the Bedford Corners Hotel, a small hotel near Tottenham Court and Oxford Street, two blocks from the British Museum and within walking distance of the theater district and the London School of Economics. This was an excellent location for us to see the sights and to take in some plays. After lunch on Sunday we walked around the area to get ourselves oriented. We then rested in our hotel room and went out to a Chinese restaurant in Soho for dinner. I was almost enjoying myself. On Monday we decided to get some theater tickets and to visit some of the art galleries. Most of the stores were closed and to our surprise we discovered that it was a bank holiday. Nevertheless, the National Gallery, in Trafalgar Square, was open, and we did obtain theater tickets for Monday night. I sat through the play but had difficulty concentrating. My depression caused me to be too preoccupied with myself. Yet seeing the play was not a painful experience and I was able to comprehend parts of it. I was worried about my colloquium the next day and also about finding my way from our hotel to the London School of Economics (LSE). On Monday afternoon, my wife and I did a "dry run" from our hotel to LSE. After the play we went to a very nice restaurant.

I was invited to lunch with the Chairman of the Psychology Department of LSE on Tuesday, May 30, before my talk. To my pleasant surprise we were joined by a former professor of mine from the University of Illinois, who was now on sabbatical at LSE, on leave from Stanford University. My talk went very well (although I was not really convinced that it did), and I subsequently received a most complimentary and flattering letter from the Chairman of the Psychology Department. I walked back to the hotel from LSE all by myself without difficulty. That night my wife and I went to another play, but I again had difficulty concentrating on the plot. I did, however, understand parts of it. After the play we went to Peter Mario's, an excellent Italian restaurant. We returned to Oxford by train on Wednesday.

One of the graduate students in psychology at Oxford was a Canadian, and he and his wife invited us to their college for dinner on Thursday night (June 1). Oxford revolves around the college system, and unless one is affiliated with a college, life can be very boring. Michael Argyle had arranged for me to be a visiting Fellow at Wolfson College in which he was actively involved and I went there for lunch with him several times. In fact, both of us went to the college to a visitors' night dinner, with our wives, on Friday, June 2. It was a charming and interesting experience. Both my wife and I love a large city, like Toronto, in which we live. At Oxford there are few activities that are independent of the college system. It is extremely difficult for a four-week visitor to become integrated into the social life of the town. Both my wife and I were bored silly. This certainly didn't help my depression. Had I not been depressed, we probably would have taken more side trips, for example to Bath or Scotland. Had the environment been more stimulating I might not have been so preoccupied with my depression. My wife was a real stoic while at Oxford!

After my final talk on Tuesday, June 6 (which I presented after experiencing an anxiety attack), my wife and I took the Argyles out to dinner at the "Bear Hotel," a famous restaurant and inn in Woodstock, near Oxford. Before that we had visited Blenheim Palace (in Woodstock) and Winston Churchill's grave nearby.

Michael took us to the Oxford station Thursday morning, June 8, and we took the train to Reading and the bus to Heathrow Airport. We arrived in Toronto on Thursday evening and our son picked us up at the airport. He informed us that my in-laws, who were visiting at our house in Toronto, were planning to move from Montreal to Toronto at the beginning of August. They would be living a few blocks from our house. This would be very nice for them and I was pleased.

The next morning I was exhausted and had difficulty waking up. The combination of jet lag and my depression were not conducive to an alert altitude. I phoned Dr. Persad and arranged to see him on Monday, June 12. The weekend was uneventful, except for seeing some of our friends. I saw Dr. Persad on Monday and told him that I was still depressed and anxious and that I still felt incompetent and inadequate. He thought that I was in much better shape than I thought I was. The objective evidence was that I had presented a number of talks at Oxford, had consulted with graduate students about research, and had done it well. He recommended an increase in the dosage of the medication because the level of medication I had taken at Oxford was merely a "holding operation" and was not a therapeutically effective dose. The level of Elavil was gradually increased from 75 to 150 mg and that of Valium from 20 to 30 mg.

I saw Dr. Persad again the week of June 19 and again in the week of June 26. He was surprised that I was still anxious. He was concerned that I had become adapted to the Valium and worried lest I might become (psychologically) addicted to it. Therefore he switched me to a stronger antianxiety drug, namely, lorazepam (trade name Ativan, a benzodiazepine with central nervous system depressant properties). After taking some Ativan I really felt better and for the first time in three months wanted to drive the car. We visited some friends on the Friday night. I drove and a number of times I almost climbed the curb. Luckily my wife warned me about it. The next morning I felt like playing tennis and drove to the tennis court with my cousin's husband. Again, I almost mounted the sidewalk without being aware of it. My cousin's husband became concerned. He was also disturbed by my lack of coordination on the tennis court—without my being aware or concerned about it. When we got home he told my wife about it and she refused to let me drive again until we talked to Dr. Persad. We phoned him on Monday. It turned out that he had inadvertently prescribed too much Ativan: 12

mg a day (4 mg, three times a day) instead of 6 mg a day (2 mg three times a day). When this was corrected, my coordination was much improved but it wasn't normal. (Some of the possible side effects of Ativan are drowsiness, dizziness, fatigue, lethargy, disorientation, blurred vision, and *depression*. But it sure alleviates anxiety.)

By mid-July I was beginning to feel a bit better and even tried to play tennis once or twice. My coordination was not up to my usual standards, however, Dr. Persad thought that I was in much better shape than I believed myself to be. He also felt that I was my own worse critic. He said I was doing fine, but I felt that I was functioning at "half-mast." My wife and I socialized and went to Stratford to see *Macbeth*. I started to make plans for the fall. During the third week in July, Dr. Persad suggested that I start taking lithium. He was convinced that I had a bipolar affective disorder and was concerned that I might be becoming high. I did not think so, but I thought that a dose of the lithium was a good idea and I readily agreed. He started me off with two capsules a day (300 mg a capsule) and then increased it to three capsules a day (a total of 900 mg a day). He suggested capsules rather than tablets because the capsules are easier to swallow and are also less harmful to the digestive system.

Because the effective dose of lithium is fairly close to the toxic dose, it is necessary to test the blood plasma level for toxicity. Therefore periodic blood tests are necessary for people who take lithium. Although it is primarily an antimanic agent, it is believed that it can also have a prophylactic effect against depression. We discuss some of the technical aspects and general theories and issues of lithium in Chapter 10. At this point I should like to discuss the effect it had on me.

After about two weeks on lithium (which I was taking in conjunction with Elavil and Ativan) I developed a hand tremor. This was most pronounced when I was stirring coffee or tea, eating soup, or playing tennis. My coordination on the tennis court was awful. I knew exactly where and how I wanted to hit the ball but I just couldn't do it. I felt uncomfortable driving. After a few weeks the tremor subsided slightly, but I still had difficulty playing tennis. I also felt as if I were on a leash. Dr. Persad decreased the lithium dose to two tablets a day (600 mg) and the tremor gradually disappeared. My tennis improved slightly and I felt more comfortable driving my car.

Dr. Persad went away on vacation in mid-August and asked me to see Dr. Stancer. I told Dr. Stancer that I was still anxious and he increased the dose of Elavil from 150 to 175 mg and then to 200 mg.

At the end of August the American Psychological Association (APA) held its annual convention in Toronto and I saw many old friends. Except for some slight difficulty in urinating, a dry mouth, some mild anxiety, poor coordination, and a general feeling of restraint, I was my old self. Visiting with old friends at APA was an exhilarating experience.

Dr. Persad reduced the dosage of Elavil from 200 to 175 mg and then to 150 mg during September. I had been functioning as chairman at some level since mid- or late June and at top level since the beginning of August. My "tennis game" came back about two weeks after the lithium dosage had been reduced from three capsules (900 mg) to two capsules (600 mg) a day. During August I had had periodontal (gum) surgery but it didn't affect my psychological well being. I did give up my pipe, which I had enjoyed from the time I was 16, and have not smoked since. My mouth was still dry but this was caused by the Elavil. I ate sugarless mints and/or Certs to counteract the mouth dryness. My wife felt that I had lost my ebullience, but I believe that even this had been restored by March or April of 1979.

My first depression was alleviated dramatically and instantaneously by ECT. My second depression took much longer to dissipate. I suffered no depression in April 1979 nor in April 1980. As I rewrite this chapter it is early April 1981 and I feel fine, but I am still taking a maintenance dose of lithium of 600 mg a·day. Like a diabetic takes insulin for diabetes, I may have to take lithium for my bipolar affective disorder for the rest of my life. If I am symptom-free for another short time, I may be able to go off the lithium on a trial basis. (In actual fact, I went off the lithium on a trial basis in mid-April 1981. So far, so good!) Lithium probably acts like a fine-tuning mechanism. It fine tunes our moods. If they are too high, lithium helps to lower them. If they are too low, lithium helps to raise them. There are always trade offs in life. The prospect of having to take lithium for the rest of my life is a small price to pay for being my old cheerful, easy-going, self again. C'est la vie!

Postscript

''Norm, I never believed that the eyes were really the windows to the soul, until you were depressed.'' One of my colleagues recently said this to me after reading a draft copy of this book. She informed me that my eyes had reflected the fact when I was depressed and had signaled the fact when I was well. My wife told me that my eyes looked sunken, dead, and haunted when I was depressed and had regained their sparkle and twinkle when I felt better. Dr Persad knew by my eyes that I was getting better during the course of the ECT. The eyes, at least in my case, reflected my illness and my recuperation.

10
The Affective Disorders and Lithium

In Chapter 2 I discussed briefly the affective disorders in the sections on manic-depression and depression in history. In this chapter I describe and discuss the various categories of the affective disorders, theories of depression, and the role of lithium in the treatment of manic-depression. In the mid-1970s the American Psychiatric Association set up a Task Force on Nomenclature and Statistics, chaired by Robert Spitzer, whose main task was to revise the psychiatric diagnostic system. The official classification manual, effective July 1980 (delayed from January 1980), is the Diagnostic and Statistical Manual of Mental Disorders (DSM-III). Until then the DSM-II was used. In the DSM-III some of the categories of the DSM-II were dropped and new ones were added. The classification is based in part on research, in part on clinical observation, and in part on politics; for example, many psychologists believe that psychiatry is trying to gain complete control of diagnosis and treatment by defining all emotional problems as primarily medical in nature. It is still too early, however, to pass final judgment.

The DSM-II had a complete classification scheme for the affective disorders and included three major diagnostic categories; namely, major affective disorders, depressive neurosis, and psychotic depressive reaction. The major affective disorders include the manic-depressive illnesses (including mania, depression, and manic-depression) and involutional melancholia (change of life depression).

The *neurotic* and *psychotic depressive reaction* categories of DSM-II are distinguished from the *major affective disorders* (e.g., manic-depression, depressed type) partly by the fact that for the first two categories an environmental event is believed to have induced the depression. But this distinction is easier "said" than "done." It sounds nice in theory but in practice it is often difficult to implement it.

Analogous, to some extent, to this distinction is the threefold distinction of depression in terms of various causes, namely, endogenous, reactive, and neurotic. *Endogenous depression* is believed to be due to the malfunctioning of the physiological, biochemical, and central nervous system (including the brain) processes and structures. Depression is due to internal factors. This is analogous to the depression subcategory of the major affective disorders of DSM-II. *Reactive depression* is caused by events external to the person. It is related to a loss that influences the person's future and well-being. It is a grief reaction. *Neurotic depression* is a function of a basic maladjustment in personality functioning. Here the depression is due to a failure of the person to adapt to the stresses of day-to-day life. Exhaustion here is due to a failure to deal with severe stress and/or stress of a long duration. Depression here is the same as the neurotic depression of DSM-II.

Whereas the DSM-II categorized the affective disorders on the basis of the presence of psychosis and called all major affective disorders psychosis, except for those brought on by stressful personal life experiences, the DSM-II organizes all the affective disorders into one general category (except for those related to an organic disturbance of known origin). There are basically three subclasses in this category: *major affective disorders, other specific affective disorders,* and *atypical affective disorders.*

Major Affective Disorders.   In the DSM-III the major affective disorders are classified as bipolar disorder or major depression. The classification of bipolar disorder is used to identify all persons who have experienced a manic episode. This is because the research evidence indicates a likelihood that persons experiencing mania eventualy experience major depressive episodes. The present episode may be further subclassified as manic, depressed, or mixed. The diagnosis of bipolar disorder, according to the DSM-III, is analogous to a manic-depressive, manic, or circular type diagnosis of the DSM-II.

The DSM-III recognizes the significant distinction between unipolar and bipolar affective disorders (based on empirical evidence). The

DSM-II classification assumed that there was a unity to manic-depressive illness. According to the DSM-III system, manic-depressive illness, depressed, is classified as major depression, with recurrent episodes indicated as a subcategory. What was called involutional melancholia in DSM-II is included in major depression in DSM-III because there is no significant evidence to indicate that depression occurring during the involutional period of life is fundamentally different from that occurring in other periods.

The DSM-III classification scheme is appreciative of the heterogeneity of major depressive episodes. Melancholia is used to designate a subcategory (frequently called *endogenous*). Melancholia is more severe; manifests classic vegetative signs and is responsive to electroconvulsive therapy.

Other Specific Affective Disorders.   These disorders involve a continuous mood disturbance that lasts at least two years. For this disorder there is no *full* affective syndrome characterized by mood and associated symptoms. There are no psychotic features.

Atypical Affective Disorders.   As a wastebasket category of the affective disorders, this group doesn't fit into *major affective disorders* or *other specific affective disorders*.

The prime distinction (within the major affective disorders), supported by strong empirical evidence, appears to be that between *bipolar affective disorder* and *unipolar depressive disorder* (major depression).

As indicated earlier, the affective disorders are primarily disturbances of mood. All of us have highs and lows in our lives. We may have the "blues" for various reasons, but these feelings are transient, as are our sad feelings when we see a gloomy movie, lose a job, or part with someone we are close to. This is not depression. Depression is an illness that pervades a person's life and seriously interferes with day-to-day functioning.

All depressions are characterized by three important factors; intensity, duration, and quality. The *intensity* of a depression may be *mild, moderate,* or *severe.* Mild depressions, although upsetting, can usually be alleviated quickly. Moderate and severe depressions are classified as serious and should be treated by a psychiatrist or psychologist. The intensity of my own depression was moderate, although at times (e.g., when I suffered side effects from the drugs and just before ECT) it verged on the severe. With respect to *duration* a depression may be acute, recurrent, or chronic. Acute depressions, independent of their cause, begin quickly and may last as little as a week or as long as four months. They can sometimes clear up spontaneously without treatment. Recurrent depressions are acute repetitive episodes that reappear at various intervals; the patient is in remission (a state of normalcy) in between. Chronic depressions begin more gradually and may last for an indefinite time, sometimes two or more years, with ultimate remission, of course. The duration of my 1977 depression was basically acute, although it did recur once in 1978. With respect to *quality* a depression may be *retarded* or *agitated.* In the retarded state the patient's functions are slowed down. In the agitated state the individual is in a state of general nervous arousal or excitement. The quality of my own depression was agitated, although at times there was some evidence of retarded affect and motor behavior.

Bipolar disorder (manic-depression) and *unipolar* depression (major depression) are major affective disorders. Both are similar to what was once called *endogenous depression,* that is, depressions that are internally generated and involve physiological, biochemical, and nervous system changes. The bipolar disorder is puzzling to the patient, family, and friends. The term *manic* refers to the high, or overstimulation of mood, which the patient exhibits. Manic feelings are the converse of depressed emotions. In a manic state the individual is "hopped up." In effect, the patient feels *too* good. Depression is feeling *low* or *bad.* The patient is, among other things, distraught, exhausted, irritable, sad, and listless. Manic-depressive or bipolar illness exists in a number of variations. In its most classic form low or depressive moods alternate with pathologically high feelings. Sometimes the high comes before a depression; sometimes it comes after. A full bipolar cycle consists of a high and low period.

In manic-depression there are frequent recurring phases of depression or mania which may be acute or chronic. There can also be mixed and unpredictable cycles. For some people depressive episodes may recur, with the absence of a high period in between. This would be diagnosed as manic-depressive, *depressed*. For other people manic or high episodes may recur, with the absence of low or depressed periods in between. This would be diagnosed as manic-depressive, *manic*.

The median age for the onset of the first depression is 30. It can, however, appear as early as 20 or as late as 40. Both sexes are equally susceptible to bipolar affective disorders. A second episode may appear to be a repeat of the first. A subsequent one may be more severe or milder in its intensity than a earlier one. Acute episodes may last a week to four months. Chronic episodes may last a year or more before remission. A remission may last three or four months to 15 years. Sometimes a remission will last indefinitely. Some patients may have as few as two episodes of recurrent acute depression, whereas others (and this is rare) may suffer through 10 or more. It is part of the nature of the bipolar affective disorders that there is a pattern of remission and recurrence. It is hoped that the advent of the use of lithium will serve as a prophylactic and prevent the recurrence of mania and of depression.

With proper intensive treatment and luck the first depression usually lasts four to six weeks. Dr. Stancer told me that I was the unluckiest patient he had ever met in terms of side effects from drugs. Some patients will have side effects with one drug but not with another. Rarely will a patient encounter side effects with all drugs. I did! Therefore my first depression lasted three to four months. In general, if a depression is untreated, a patient may remain depressed for three months to two years, unless, of course, the condition deteriorates and the patient suicides. This was not a factor in my depression.

What happens if and when the second depression occurs? The possibility of a second depression was furthest from my mind when my first depression lifted in September 1977. It is true that I was *hypomanic* for about two months (from mid-September to mid-November) and was possessed of a great deal of energy, ideas, and plans (*hypo* means "less than," and therefore hypomania means less than mania). But by mid-November I was "normal." I knew there was a possibility of recurrence, but I wasn't going to worry about it. I guess no one likes to live with the "Sword of Damocles" hanging over his head. So possibly I was being defensive by not worrying about the possibility of a recurrence of my depression.

Therefore I went about my business as if I had never been depressed.

When my depression recurred in April 1978 I didn't say, "Gee whiz! Here we go again!" Instead, because of our experience with the first depression my wife and I recognized the early warning symptoms of the second depression. These symptoms included anxiety, irritation, tension, fatigue, difficulty in sleeping (e.g., early morning waking), loss of appetite, loss of sex drive, sadness and inadequacy, and lack of concentration. Therefore I called Dr. Persad promptly and was given immediate treatment. Had it not been necessary for me to go to Oxford, I would have been able to have continuous, uninterrupted treatment in May 1978 and my depression would have been alleviated earlier. As it was, because I sought treatment at once, my second depression was not so severe as my first and I suffered less.

Theories of Depression

What causes depression? What are the factors involved? Why are some people depressed and others are not? Both psychological and physiological factors have been implicated in the etiology of the affective disorders and some attempts have been made to supply sociological explanations. Some theories emphasize psychological factors and ignore the physiological, whereas other theories do the reverse. Some emphasize sociological perspectives. Before discussing the psychological, sociological, and physiological theories of depression, I should like to say something about *endogenous* versus *exogenous* (reactive) depression.

Earlier I mentioned the common distinction made between endogenous and exogenous or reactive depression and pointed out that endogenous depression refers to a disorder that originates in the body; that is, it is believed by some that endogenous depression is caused by a physiological malfunction. Exogenous (or reactive) depression pertains to causes originating outside the body and is due to environmental factors; that is, *reactive* defines the nature of this type of depression.

What is the validity of the distinction between endogenous and exogenous (reactive) depression? If this distinction were valid, then those depressed persons diagnosed as reactive or exogenous would have suffered through more environmental stresses just before the onset of their depression than depressed persons diagnosed as endogenous. This is not the case, however, as shown empirically by Drs. Leff, Roatch, and Bunney in 1970 and by Drs. Akiskal and McKinney in 1975. Because of the difficulties of distinguishing endogenous from exogenous empirically, the distinction has been reconceptualized. The labels no longer refer to the absence or presence of precipitating environmental events but rather to different patterns of behavior. Endogenous patients are more likely than exogenous patients to manifest deep depression, motor retardation, loss of interest in life, lack of reaction to the environment, middle of the night insomnia, no self-pity, and bodily symptoms. This endogenous versus exogenous distinction is still a controversial one. Some clinicians and scientists believe that, analogous to the psychotic-neurotic distinction, it reflects the degree of severity (endogenous is more severe than exogenous) and is not a typology.

Psychological Theories of Depression.   Three psychological theories of depression are *psychoanalytic, cognitive,* and *learning.* Probably the earliest theories were *psychoanalytic.* Abraham, a student of Freud's and a psychoanalyst, presented the first psychoanalytic theory of depression in 1911, and Freud published his own view of depression in a famous paper entitled "Mourning and Melancholia" in 1917. Abraham attempted to distinguish between normal grief and abnormal depression. The main theme for both Abraham and Freud was that self-centeredness differentiated depression from normal grief. Depression focuses on the self, whereas grief focuses on others. According to Freud, the seeds of depression are planted early in childhood. The child may be frustrated or overindulged at the oral stage and thus becomes "fixated" at that stage. If the child is fixated at the oral stage it becomes overly dependent on others for developing and maintaining self-esteem and self-worth and meeting psychological needs.

How can fixation at the oral stage in childhood lead to depression in adulthood? After a person suffers the loss (through separation or death) of a loved one the lost person is mourned and unconsciously introjected (incorporated) as a means of "undoing" the loss. All of us have mixed or ambivalent feelings toward those with whom we have close relationships. If we also hate the lost person that we love and we identify with or introject that person, we direct some of the hate or anger inward toward ourselves. Following the introjection and concomitant resentment and guilt, there is the mourning. Now the mourner recalls memories of the one who is gone and separates him- or herself from that lost person.

This is the normal process of grief. For those who are overly dependent a process of self-blame, self-abuse, and depression may ensue. They cannot wean themselves emotionally from the individual who has died or left and they continue to blame themselves for the bad points and faults perceived in the loved (and lost) individual who has been introjected. The anger toward the lost one remains directed inward and this, according to psychoanalysis, is the basis of *depression*. Because depression is related to the loss of a loved one, psychoanalysis had to introduce the concept of symbolic loss, to account for the depression in which no actual loss has occurred.

A number of problems appear in the psychoanalytic formulation of depression; for example, because the mourner both hates and loves the lost one, why is only hate (and anger) turned inward and why not love? Why not introject love and be a happy person instead of hate and being a depressed person? Another problem is in connection with a fixation that Freud says is due to too much or too little gratification. How much gratification is good? "Symbolic loss" is also a problem; it can always be invoked *post hoc*. This is the classic psychoanalytic interpretation of depression. Of course, much has been written since Freud and Abraham, but it is beyond the scope of this book.

The cognitive theories propose that cognitive processes are important determinants of emotional behavior. Research on feelings of helplessness and the work and theorizing of Albert Ellis on irrational beliefs provide some support for this notion. The most significant modern cognitive theory of depression is that originally proposed by Aaron T. Beck in 1967. Beck, a psychiatrist at the University of Pennsylvania, believes that depressed patients feel depressed because they commit characteristic *logical errors* in thinking. They perceive the world about them in terms of self-blame and catastrophes; for example, a normal person might interpret a snowstorm as an inconvenient and irritating event, but a depressed patient would interpret this event as another indication of the futility and hopelessness of life. Depressives are not illogical in general, but they do draw illogical conclusions when it comes to evaluating themselves.

According to Beck, these *errors in thinking* are *schemata* or characteristic sets that bias the individual's perceptions of the world.

The major schemata for a depressed person are those of *self-blame* and *self-deprecation*. This type of person would label events in terms of "What an idiot I am" or "Everything is useless." Beck points to at least four logical errors that depressed people are prone to commit when assessing the real world: *overgeneralization, selective abstraction, magnification and minimization,* and *arbitrary inference*.

Beck's cognitive theory is different from most other theories of depression; for example, many theorists, including Freud, perceive depressives as victims of their emotions, so distraught that their intellectual capabilities cannot control or influence their feelings. Beck takes the opposite position. He believes that our emotional reactions are due to how we conceptualize the world and that the perceptions of depressed persons are not congruent with the real world. Persons suffering from depression make illogical judgments about themselves. They perceive neither themselves nor the world about them realistically.

Do depressed patients actually judge themselves in more illogical ways than nondepressed persons? Beck, on the basis of clinical observations, has noted that depressives do show the logical errors in the interpretation of reality that we have discussed. Does the misperception or false cognition cause the depression, or are the cognitive errors a function of some primary emotional disturbance or even due to a third factor such as biochemical malfunctioning? It is true that an individual's emotions can be influenced by how she or he perceives situations and people. There is no evidence to indicate that the noncognitive or emotional aspects of depression are secondary to or due to inappropriate cognitive schemata, as suggested by Beck. At the moment all we can state is that depression and cognitive disturbances coexist, but no specific causal relationship has been demonstrated. It is possible that cognitions influence emotions or vice versa or even that both processes coexist. It is even possible that both cognitive and emotional disturbances are caused by biochemical imbalances.

Learning theories of depression present varying points of view. They do not represent a homogenized unitary position. Some bear a resemblance to Freud's theory of depression. You may recall that Freud suggested that one causal factor in depression was the loss of a loved one, either by death or separation, especially for those persons who had strong oral dependencies (fixated at the oral stage) and who were vulnerable to diminution of support by significant others. Another way of putting it is to say that with the loss of a significant other there is a withdrawal and loss of an important source of positive reinforcement. There is then a withdrawal from certain activities by the depressed persons.

Some learning theories have proposed a theory of depression that is related to a *reduction in reinforcement* (reward); for example, after a loss people will change their behavior because of a decrease in reinforcement possibilities, but the newer and lower level of activity itself may be reinforced. People who are depressed usually receive sympathy or special attention from friends, relatives, and colleagues. These significant others do not now expect too much from the depressed person. Therefore the lower level of activity is rewarded. There is less probability and possibility of improvement, especially for those persons who lack the social skills for making new contacts (friends, hobbies, etc.) to compensate for the activities they engaged in with the person they lost. There is some confirmation of the theory (proposed by P. M. Lewinshohn and his associates) that depression is related to low rates of positively reinforced behavior. At present, however, a specific causal relationship between reinforcement and mood has not yet been proved.

Martin Seligman has presented a *learned helplessness* model of depression that basically provides a cognitive learning point of view. Anxiety and depression, according to Seligman, grow and develop in feelings of helplessness, and these feelings are learned. Anxiety is the first reaction to a stressful situation. This anxiety is replaced by depression if the individual believes that the situation is uncontrollable and learns to perceive the situation as helpless, a situation that cannot be dealt with. Seligman's model, unlike Lewinshohn's, is a *cognitive* one. He examines the way in which the person learns to conceptualize the relationships between activity and outcome; that is, the person may perceive that he or she is helpless and that all efforts to cope with a problem are useless. Seligman has conducted research with both animals and humans.

He believes that learned helplessness is *analogous* to depression. His theory suggests that the roots of depression are in learning. So may be its treatment and cure. If people can be put in situations in which they learn to exert greater control over their environment, their depression may be alleviated. Note that the learned helplessness studies are *analogues* for depression. Even the depressed college students that

Seligman has used as subjects function at a fairly high and effective level. Nevertheless, his research is promising in terms of attempting to understand the etiology and of suggesting some useful strategies for treating depression.

Learned helplessness and *depression* have some similarities in terms of *symptoms* (e.g., passivity, negative cognitive set, norepinephrine depletion, weight loss, and social and sexual deficits), *cure* (norepinephrine, ECT, and time), and *causes* (believing that responding is useless). If, however, depression is also due to physiological and biochemical factors, then there are also some important differences between learned helplessness and depression.

Sociological Perspectives. Some attempts have been made to implicate sociological factors in the affective disorders, especially with respect to suicide. The sociocultural and sociopolitical factors that are related to the affective disorders have no simple and direct effects but are mediated by other variables. Mass communication variables, for example, by themselves, or an exposure to them would not normally lead to alienation and suicide. When the Toronto newspapers stopped dramatizing those suicides that were committed by persons jumping in front of subway trains, these suicides decreased dramatically. Seeing a sad or pathetic play on television may make someone who is depressed more depressed; that is, a mass communication variable may interact with a personal variable and exacerbate pathological behavior. The mass media, especially television, may provide models that viewers may emulate or identify with.

Émile L. Durkheim, the eminent French sociologist, in his classic book *Suicide* (1897), noted that a sense of *anomie* (being without norms or standards) and *alienation,* that is, separation, isolation, and unrelatedness, were prevalent in those societies in which suicide rates were high. One important characteristic of adjustment and happiness is a sense that one belongs and is needed and wanted by others. In our modern society sociological, psychological, and political changes have not kept up with technological changes. We suffer from what Alvin Toffler has called *Future Shock.* Because of the vast technological changes and because we are often treated like numbers and objects, rather than like subjects, we often feel that we do not count, that we do not belong. We feel alienated and this can exacerbate feelings of depression. As noted later in this chapter, it is my belief that the physical, metabolic, and biochemical disturbances of the nervous system are heavily implicated in the major affective disorders.

With respect to social class and mental illness, August B. Hollingshead and F.C. Redlich (1958) found in their well known study that neurotic depression was twice as prevalent in the upper social classes, compared with the lower. The nonneurotic depressions (the major affective disorders) were two and one half times more frequent in the lower classes compared with the upper. In a comparison of rural versus urban populations E. G. Jaco (1960) found that involutional depressions occur twice as frequently in the urban areas in Texas. B. Malzberg (1962) has noted that in the United States Jews suffer more frequently from the affective disorders than non-Jews.

A.J. Marsella (1979) has recently reviewed the cross-cultural literature with respect to depression. The frequency with which depression and mania occur varies among different societies. In some societies manic manifestations are more prevalent, whereas in other societies depressive manifestations are more prevalent. In the North American culture, in general, schizophrenia is more prevalent than (or at least diagnosed more frequently than) manic-depression; in the Hutterite culture manic-depression is more prevalent than schizophrenia. In general, the Hutterites have a fairly low rate of mental illness and an extremely high recovery rate. About 30 years ago J. C. Carothers found that mania was common among the East Africans that he studied but that depressive disorders were rare. In the United States, at that time the reverse was true. Obviously there have been many changes since the early 1950s, and more recent observations provide a different pattern. As underdeveloped societies adopt some of the values of the more "advanced" and "progressive" American and western European culture, their people are more likely to develop western style affective disorders; that is, depression based on personal responsibility for failure and misfortune, depression facilitated by stress, and depression associated with guilt and self-recrimiation.

In nonindustrialized societies, for example, among the Australian aborigines, there is an absence of self-recrimination and guilt associated with depression, and attempted or actual suicide is quite rare. In some non-Western cultures the symptoms are basically nonpsychological and include vegetative characteristics such as weight loss, anorexia, difficulty in sleeping, and a loss of sex drive. A.J. Marsella found that in some cultures the *concept* of depression as we know it doesn't exist. One of the major difficulties with cross-cultural studies is that the diagnostic procedures are not always comparable. J. E. Cooper and his colleagues (1972) compared psychiatric diagnoses in New York and London and found that the concepts of schizophrenia and depression are somewhat different in the United States and England. Professor Joseph Zubin, a psychologist, found that many cases diagnosed as schizophrenia in the United States were labeled as depressive and manic-depressive in England and vice-versa. Another difficulty with the cross-cultural studies is that there is often no clear distinction between reactive and endogenous depression; therefore reactive depression in one culture may possibly be compared with endogenous depression in another. Therefore the cross-cultural results should be interpreted cautiously.

Professor George W. Brown, a sociologist, and his colleagues at Bedford College, London, have been examining the role of social factors in psychiatric disorders. In collaboration with psychiatrists from the Medical Research Council Social Psychiatry Unit, based at Maudsley Hospital, they investigated the influences of social factors on depression (see *Social Origins of Depression: A Study of Psychiatric Disorders in Women* by G. W. Brown and T. Harris, London: Tavistock Publications, 1978). Brown and Harris conducted an extensive investigation of 114 female psychiatric patients and 458 women randomly selected from the population of the London borough of Camberwell (a lower class community). They implied that all depression is caused primarily by *psychosocial factors,* such as major life events, including those involving loss by death and those involving loss by separation, and by *vulnerability factors,* which increase the probability of depression in the presence of precipitating factors such as loss. In their sample vulnerability factors included the absence of close ties or of employment, the presence of three or more children under 14 and the loss of the mother before the age of 11. They point out that there are social factors that *trigger* the onset of depression as opposed to those that are more directly *causal.*

One of the major points that Brown and Harris make is that social influences may play a significant role in depression and therefore should be taken into account. They believe that drug treatment such as antidepressants are unlikely to be adequate by themselves. They recommend social therapy, aimed at raising self-esteem, as an adjunct to drug therapy. Brown and Harris believe that more pervasive political and social changes can decrease the base rate of depression by minimizing the occurrence of vulnerability factors.

Although they emphasize the social disease aspect of depression, it is important to note that their studies were retrospective and do not answer the important question why many women who are exposed to stressful life events and vulnerability factors do not become depressed. Genetic factors are important, especially for patients with bipolar manic-depressive affective disorders. Note that only three of the 114 patients investigated by Brown and Harris were bipolar manic-depressives. Although social factors and psychological factors play a role in the etiology and reactions to depressions, biological and genetic factors seem to have a preeminent role in the bipolar affective disorders.

With respect to sociocultural variables in our North American culture it seems that conditions that increase the stress of life increase the frequency of the reactive affective disorders and may exaggerate the depressive symptoms of the major effective (bipolar and unipolar) disorders. Reactive depressions seem to occur more frequently among the divorced than among the married and more frequently in urban than in rural areas. Depression may also be higher in the upper socioeconomic classes than in the lower. Methodological difficulties of the various studies and diagnostic biases make it difficult to draw firm conclusions.

Suicide and Sociocultural Factors.   Suicide, a possible concomitant of the affective disorders, is also related to sociocultural factors. Protestants commit suicide about seven times more frequently than Catholics. Suicide is more frequent in urban centers than in rural communities, and within both groups it is more prevalent for upper and middle class persons than for the lower class. Émile Durkheim, in 1897, noted that in several countries in Europe the male suicide rate was four times as common as the female suicide rate. Although today this four-to-one gap has narrowed, males still commit suicide more frequently than females, at least in North America and Europe.

There has been a frightening increase in teenage suicides since 1960 or 1965. Perhaps this is related to increased teenage frustration and alienation in dealing with a world that is not of their making. The suicide rate is also high among American Indians. Perhaps Indian youth face major difficulties in integrating their Indian heritage with the modern-day world. If the young Indian decides to remain on the reservation, he has no real way to support his family. If, however, he leaves the reservation, he must give up his culture and traditions and is in no way guaranteed that he will succeed economically.

Changes in the organization of a social group profoundly affect the frequency of depression and suicide. Social disorganization is positively related to suicide; for example, American Indians who have shown a dramatic increase in suicide during the last few decades have suffered from economic deprivation and have been in conflict between assimilation into the majority society and maintaining their own cultural integrity. Upward social mobility is also positively related to the frequency of suicide. Although the sociocultural factors are important to an understanding of the affective disorders, they are probably peripheral compared with the more central biochemical factors.

Physiological and Biochemical Theories of Depression. In this section I focus on the genetic and biochemical factors related to depression. Physiological processes, especially the arousal levels of the autonomic nervous system (the sympathetic and parasympathetic nervous systems), have a profound effect on our emotions, hence on our moods. Therefore it is not surprising that scientists and clinicians have attempted to find some physiological bases for depression and mania and have attempted to relate physiological malfunctioning to genetic factors.

In effect, there are at least two potential sources of evidence for the physiological basis of depression; *genetic data* and *biochemical evidence*. Much of the research on the role of *genetic* factors in depression has focused on twin and family studies and has been concerned with bipolar disorders and unipolar major depression (the major affective disorders). As you may recall, bipolar refers to persons who have suffered episodes of depression and mania, whereas unipolar refers to persons who have suffered only episodes of depression.

With respect to base rates, it is estimated that about 1 to 2 percent of the population suffer from bipolar depression. (About 5 percent of men and 9 percent of women will experience an affective disorder at sometime in their lives.) The morbidity rate for first-degree relatives of bipolars is significantly higher and ranges from 10 to 20 percent. Furthermore, the relatives of the bipolar depressives are not at high risk for unipolar depression. This provides additional support for the distinction between unipolar and bipolar depression. The concordance data for depression rates of identical twins is quite impressive; for example, Zerbin-Rudin found that the overall concordance rate (rate of agreement, i.e., if one twin is depressed, the probability of the other twin being depressed is the concordance rate) for depression was 70 percent, and most of the ill cotwins were bipolar depressives (i.e., if one twin was depressed, in 70 percent of the cases the identical cotwin was also depressed). With respect to fraternal, or nonidentical, twins, the concordance rate for bipolar depression, according to Price, is only 23 percent. More than half the bipolar depressions recur, independent of environmental stress. All these data strongly suggest that bipolar depression is, to a certain extent, due to *genetic* factors; that is, bipolar depression has an inheritable component. Definitive studies have not yet been conducted in this area.

George Winokur and his colleagues at the University of Iowa have postulated that bipolar depression is due to a dominant gene on the X chromosome. The X chromosome is one of two chromosomes that, taken together, determine sex. There are 46 chromosomes in humans, or 23 pairs. Women have an XX or a similar pair of sex chromosomes; men have a dissimilar pair, XY. If a gene is dominant, it will be independent 'of the other gene with which it is paired. The mother always contributes an X chromosome to the offspring, the father an X or a Y. If the father contributes an X chromosome, the child will be a girl; if a Y, the child will be a boy.

The family histories of patients manifesting affective disorders were investigated by Winokur and his coworkers. Winokur then separates the patients into two groups, those whose families had a high degree of affective disorders and those who families did not. For the "high incidence" group 96 percent of 112 probands (original designated patients) were bipolars; in the "low incidence" group only 3 percent of 120 probands were bipolars. What this means is that the relatives of bipolar probands are at high risk of bipolar depression.

Winokur and his colleagues then attempted to cross-validate his theory and studied a new sample of 89 cases. They found that female relatives were much more likely to be depressed than male relatives.

This would support Winokur's prediction that bipolar depression is regulated by a dominant gene on the X chromosome. Among the designated bipolar depressed patients (the probands) 55 percent of the mothers, only 17 percent of the fathers, 52 percent of the sisters, and only 29 percent of the brothers were also bipolars. There was no incidence of father-son pairs of manic-depressives; there were 13 cases of father-daughter manic-depressives, 17 cases of mother-son manic-depressives, and 17 cases of mother-daughter manic-depressives. This, too, supports Winokur's theory. The gene that causes manic-depression in a father is an X chromosome. However, he passes on only his Y chromosome to his male offspring. Therefore he cannot transmit bipolar depression to his son. Winokur also found that a high proportion of male manic-depressives were color-blind (color blindness is also a sex-linked trait). He suggests that the bipolar affective disorders are sex-linked on the X chromosome and are genetically transmitted. (It should be noted that a disproportionate number of bipolars are also left-handed.)

Although Winokur's own data support his theory, studies by others (e.g., Goetzl and his colleagues; Hays) have provided evidence dissonant to that found by Winokur; for example, these other investigations have found cases of father-son pairs of bipolar depressives. Winokur's theory, although interesting, needs more intensive investigation and will probably need extensive revision, modification, and elaboration.

The research on unipolar depression has not been so extensive as that on bipolar depression. We do, however, know that although genetic factors play some role in unipolar depression they lack the impact that they have in bipolar depression. Perris found that only 7.4 percent of the first-degree relatives of unipolar depressives had also experienced a depressive episode (compared with 10 to 20 percent for bipolars). Winokur and his colleagues found similar results and also found that the relatives of unipolar depressives (especially those who became depressed at an early age) were at high risk for other behavior disorders, primarily sociopathic behavior and alcoholism.

In Chapter 6 on drugs I discussed the role of *biochemical factors* in depression and the reader is referred to that chapter. Basically the material in Chapter 6 pointed to two theories, that depression is due to low levels of norepinephrine (or noradrenaline) and/or low levels of serotonin at the synaptic gap. The norepinephrine theory also suggsts that mania is due to an excess of norepinephrine. Both norepinephrine and serotonin are neurotransmitters. I have discussed the role of antidepressants in treating the affective disorders as well as the role of ECT. Now, in this chapter I discuss lithium as a method of treatment for manic-depression.

It is my contention that the major affective disorders, that is, bipolar manic-depression and unipolar recurrent depression, are physical, metabolic, and biochemical disturbances of the nervous system. These disturbances produce changes in the brain, which subsequently produce changes in perception, cognition, reasoning ability, mood, and behavior. Psychological and physiological factors interact and are interwoven. There is no doubt that the reactions to a primary depression are psychological (as well as physiological), and the manner in which a person reacts is to a certain extent influenced by his or her premorbid personality, which accentuates both positive and negative features. The psychological factors no doubt serve as a feedback mechanism and consequently produce additional physiological changes.

There are individual differences in level of mood. Biological rhythms are analogous to daily and seasonal weather rhythms. Some individuals operate at a higher level of energy than others, and the line between normal and hypomanic behavior is sometimes a thin one. One should conceptualize moods in terms of "bands" with lower and higher "normal" levels rather than fixed points.

Whereas the major affective disorders (bipolar and unipolar) are primary and physical in origin, reactive depression and neurotic depression are secondary and psychological. Antidepressant drugs and lithium therapy are most effective for those depressions and manic-depressions that are caused by biochemical imbalance in the nervous system. The primary chemical depressions are basically different from the secondary depressions that are due to stress or caused by neurosis. Therefore a correct and precise diagnosis is essential. Although psychoanalysis, operant conditioning, cognitive reappraisal, and the teaching of coping techniques may be effective for reactive and neurotic depression are secondary and psychological. Antidepressant drugs and antidepressant drug therapy, lithium or ECT) when it comes to treating the primary or major affective disorders of bipolar manic-depression and unipolar depression. For the major affective disorders the physical therapies are the treatment of choice. Of course, they can and should be supplemented by psychological forms of therapy. Let us now turn to a discussion of the role of lithium as a treatment method.

Lithium

Ronald R. Fieve, a psychiatrist, pioneered the use of lithium in the treatment of the bipolar affective disorders in North America. He has suggested that it was not until the advent of lithium that there has been any success in bringing the affective disorders under control for any lengthy period. Dr. Fieve believes that lithium not only controls and prevents the recurrence of debilitating and chronic changes in mood (from high to low, to high, etc.), characteristic of manic-depression, but that it is also effective in preventing recurrent unipolar depression; that is, lithium serves as a *prophylactic* against bipolar manic-depression and unipolar depression. It serves to provide a "fine tuning" for our moods.

During the second century A.D. (about 1800 years ago) Soranus of Ephesus, a physician, prescribed mineral water therapy for melancholic and manic patients who were housed in the Roman and Greek tent hospitals. Soranus proposed the use of specific alkaline springs for various mental and physical illnesses. It is now known that many of the alkaline springs that the Romans developed in western and southern Europe possess a fair amount of lithium.

Lithium, the lightest of the IA group in the Periodic Table of Elements, was not discovered until 1817. John Arfvedson, the young Swedish chemistry student who discovered lithium, gave it that name because it was found in stone (*lithos* in Greek). It is one of the most reactive of all the basic elements, and even though it is never found free in nature it appears in natural brines, mineral waters, mineral rocks, and even in some human, animal, and plant tissues. Many of the spas of Europe and the United States contain lithium in the mineral waters that are offered for drinking and bathing. The presence of lithium was widely advertised during the nineteenth and early twentieth centuries, and the name Lithia was frequently given to springs (e.g., Lithia Springs, Georgia). These "Lithia" springs were promoted as purveyors of good physical and mental health (e.g., lithium when combined with uric acid can dissolve kidney stones and can be used to treat gout and rheumatism). Even today some countries believe that mineral springs can cure many different psychiatric and physical problems. In West Germany the cost of spa treatment is presently recoverable from health insurance. In the Soviet Union and Eastern Europe there are numerous state-owned spa facilities.

At the turn of the century (in the early 1900s) lithium bromide was used as a sleeping medication and for treating epilepsy. After World War II lithium chloride was a frequently used salt substitute for patients on sodium-free diets (e.g., those with heart and kidney disease) and had trade names such as Foodsal, Saltisal, and Westal. (We now know that lithium is dangerous to patients with kidney disease because some of the potential side effects of lithium are kidney problems, and it is essential that patients taking lithium have an adequate intake of regular salt. Therefore heart patients who cannot take regular salt would be prohibited from taking lithium. Those heart patients who are not suffering from *significant* cardiac conditions and do ingest regular salt can take lithium.) During 1949 many serious poisonings and at least three deaths attributed to lithium were reported. Lithium was immediately removed from the market by drug manufacturers.

In the industrial field, however, the use of lithium and lithium compounds advanced at a fast pace. It has been used in ceramics, metallurgy, and nuclear technology, and was an important compound in the hydrogen bomb. It is also used in dehumidifiers and purifiers.

As indicated earlier (see Chapter 6), John F. Cade, an Australian psychiatrist, used lithium in 1949 to treat mania. Cade's discovery was purely serendipitous, because he originally thought that urea was the toxic substance that produced manic states and urea had been found in the urine of manic patients. In his experiments he used guinea pigs as subjects. To inject them with uric acid he used lithium because it formed the most soluble salt, that is, lithium urate. To his surprise Cade found that when guinea pigs were injected with lithium urate (and later lithium carbonate) they did not become excited but instead lapsed into lethargy. He then provided 10 manics with lithium carbonate and found that it returned them to a normal mood state, so much so that some of his most chronic manics recovered enough to be discharged from the hospital (but were continued on a maintenance dose).

Shortly after John F. Cade published his results in 1949 other investigators became interested in the role of lithium in treating mania. Studies of the use of lithium salts for manics were conducted in Australia, Denmark, England, France, and Italy. Dr. Mogens Schou, in Denmark, conducted the first double-blind trial study (in 1954) in which neither the patients nor the psychiatrists knew which manics had received lithium and which had received an inert placebo. All the studies confirmed the effectiveness of lithium in treating mania.

Cade's 1949 study and Schou's 1954 study, although impressive, had no impact on the psychiatric community in the United States. One possible reason for this may be that Cade's report on lithium was published in the same year (1949) as the cardiac deaths that resulted from the misuse of lithium. The toxic and lethal level of lithium are close to its therapeutic level, and this may have frightened the American clinicians. The North American psychiatric community opted instead for the psychoactive drugs; for example, tranquilizers, phenothiazines, antidepressants, and stimulants. Finally, there was no great potential commercial value for lithium, which was a natural element and therefore could not be patented like the other psychopharmaceutical drugs. Therefore the drug companies did not "push" for the use of lithium.

The first intensive and systematic research in the United States began in 1958. Dr. Ronald R. Fieve, in conjunction with Dr. Shervert Frazier, conducted this research in the acute ward of the New York State Psychiatric Institute. In 1960 Dr. Samuel Gershon, an Australian psychiatrist who was then living in the United States, tried to persuade U.S. psychiatrists to use lithium. In the 1960s psychiatrists in Galveston, Texas, also began experiments on the use of lithium with manics. Both the New York State Psychiatric Institute study and the Texas study were presented at the American Psychiatric Association's Annual Convention in May 1965. This was the first time that the use of lithium in the treatment of mania was formally presented to the psychiatric community. Lithium went public!

During the 1960s lithium was still illegal in the United States except for research purposes. Because of the strong interest in the potential of lithium, it was suggested that the legal limitations on the marketing of this drug be reviewed. The American Psychiatric Association set up a task force on lithium in 1969. This task force assisted the U.S. Food and Drug Administration (FDA) in the preparation of a package insert which described the drug. Finally, in 1970 the FDA approved lithium as a standard prescription drug based on the recommendation of the task force. The marketing of the drug was now more conservative. At first lithium was approved only for the treatment of acute mania, but a year later in 1971 approval of its maintenance use in manic depression was recommended. Right from the beginning careful blood monitoring and rigid chemical controls were mandatory.

Since then lithium has never looked back as the drug of choice for treating acute mania and for maintenance use in manic-depression. Lithium is primarily an antimanic agent. It appears, however, that in addition to alleviating mania it acts as a prophylactic against the depressive episodes in bipolar affective disorders. If a manic depressive does become depressed, it is necessary to supplement the lithium with an antidepressant drug, for example, amitriptyline, one of the tricyclics. If monitored properly, lithium is relatively safe. The contraindications for its use include patients with *significant* cardiovascular or kidney (renal) disease and those with severe dehydration, sodium depletion, or brain damage. While taking lithium it is essential to have a normal sodium (salt) intake. Persons who are required to have a low sodium intake should not take lithium.

For the lithium therapy to be effective it is necessary to reach blood plasma levels that are fairly close to the toxic (poisonous) level. Because lithium is excreted by the kidneys, proper renal functioning is important to avoid accumulation of lithium and intoxication. Therefore a thorough clinical examination of each patient, which includes laboratory tests, blood tests, EKG, and an assessment of renal functioning, is necessary before the onset of lithium treatment.

Careful clinical and laboratory monitoring of patients is necessary in lithium treatment. Serum lithium levels should be obtained, via blood tests twice a week initially and then every month or so. As indicated earlier, lithium toxicity is closely related to serum lithium levels and therapeutic effectiveness, and during treatment the serum lithium levels should not exceed 1.5 mEq/L. Otherwise lithium intoxication and adverse reactions may occur. The lithium level typically refers to a blood sample drawn before the patient is given the first lithium dose of the day; that is, 9 to 12 hours after the last dose of the drug. To maintain lithium excretion good kidney functioning and adequate fluid and salt intake are essential.

Once the acute manic episode breaks there is a decreased tolerance to lithium. Therefore at that time the dosage should be reduced rapidly to produce serum lithium levels no higher than 0.6 to 1.2 mEq /L. During a manic episode the effective therapeutic dose should produce serum lithium levels between 1 and 1.5 mEq/L. For maintenance therapy, the level can be lower, and in some cases levels as low as 0.3 and 0.4 mEq/L have been effective.

Mild adverse effects may occur even when serum lithium values remain below 1 mEq/L. These initial side effects include gastrointestinal discomfort, nausea, vertigo, muscle weakness, and a dazed condition, which usually disappear after stabilization of therapy. The more common and persistent side effects are fine tremor of the hands and sometimes fatigue, thirst, and polyuria. These do not necessarily require a decrease in the dosage.

The dosage prescribed has to be "tailor made" for each patient and depends on the patient's clinical condition and blood concentration of lithium. Manic patients usually need serum lithium concentrations above 1 mEq/L but lower than 1.5 mEq/L. The maintenance dose, as indicated earlier, usually averages between 0.6 and 1.2 mEq/L. The suggested initial daily dosage for properly screened adult patients in a state of acute mania is 1800 mg, divided into three doses. (Lithium comes as lithium carbonate in 300 mg green tablets or 300 mg pink capsules. The capsules are more expensive but are easier to swallow and digest than the tablets.) Because of large individual differences in renal lithium excretion, it is a good idea to start lithium treatment at doses between 600 and 900 mg/day and to reach a level of 1200 to 1800 mg in divided doses on the second day.

Normally within a week the acute manic episode will disappear, and the dosage can be reduced to 600 to 900 mg/day (two or three capsules) in divided doses. The aim here is to treat the hypomania, and reach serum lithium concentration levels of 0.6 to 1.2 mEq/L. For maintenance therapy 600 to 900 mg/day, in divided doses, is usually adequate. As indicated earlier, the aim of lithium maintenance therapy is to provide "fine tuning" to our moods or affect. It is analogous to the idling of an automobile. If it idles too "quickly," we slow it down; if it idles too "slowly," we speed it up. Lithium serves this function for our moods; it "revs" them up or "revs" them down.

Dr. Ronald R. Fieve, who has done much of the pioneering work on lithium and runs the "Lithium Clinic," which originated at the New York State Psychiatric Institute and Columbia Presbyterian Medical Center, points out that the use of lithium as a specific treatment and maintenance medication for manic depression represents the first time in psychiatry that a naturally occurring salt has been capable of controlling a major mental illness. Although the tranquilizers and some of the antidepressants relieve the symptoms of anxiety and depression, they do not get at the central core of the illness. Lithium biochemically controls manic-depression and acts as a prophylactic against its recurrence. To some extent maintenance with tricyclics provides an analogous treatment for depression.

Since 1975 Dr. Fieve and his colleagues have been studying the effects of rubidium chloride on withdrawn, chronically depressed patients. Rubidium was first used on humans by S. Botkin, Jr., a Russian physician, in the 1880s. Dr. Botkin, who was a student of the famous Russian psychologist Ivan Pavlov, used rubidium on cardiac patients but noted that it was often associated with a state of well-being. One of Dr. Fieve's colleagues, Dr. Herbert Meltzer, gave rubidium to monkeys in their orange juice and found that it made them overactive and aggressive. Rubidium is a basic element closely related to lithium. It is part of the same group of alkaline metals as lithium, sodium, and potassium. Rubidium produces behavioral, biochemical and electroencephalographic effects that are opposite those of lithium. Because lithium has been demonstrated to be effective with manic episodes and as a prophylactic for some kinds of depression, it is hoped that rubidium will provide an analogous therapeutic or prophylactic function for depression. At the moment it is premature to say anything conclusive about the role of rubidium in treating depression.

The results of the use of lithium have been dramatic and exciting but also controversial. In addition to the possible dangers of toxic side effects and the fact that we do not know the long-term effects of lithium (it has been marketed only since 1970), there are political and economic controversies. Instead of undergoing long-term psychotherapy, psychoanalysis, or other kinds of "talk" therapy, a few weeks of lithium therapy are more effective, more dramatic, and far less expensive. Furthermore, once the initial diagnosis is made by a psychiatrist, it is possible to be given maintenance therapy by a GP. Much has been written about lithium. Among the sources that I have read, the one that I found the most useful is the book by Ronald R. Fieve entitled *Moodswing: The Third Revolution in Psychiatry* (published in paperback in 1975 by Bantam Books, New York).

Hypomania! Is it good or bad? Most frequently the persons who "turn you on" are hypomanic individuals. When they are not out of control and do not require treatment, they may be the superachievers in the theater, the cinema, the arts, in politics, in science, and in business. Much of this high level of energy is due to biochemical and genetic factors. With the discovery of lithium as a "fine tuner" of mood, perhaps this creativity and energy can be harnessed more constructively and effectively rather than being squandered in pathology.

11
Stigma!

It is probably more socially acceptable today, in the 1980s, to be a delinquent, drug addict, criminal, homosexual, or lesbian than to be labeled as mentally ill. The civil rights of the above groups probably receive better protection than the civil rights of mentally ill patients. In many areas mentally ill patients are still considered pariahs. Throughout history the mentally ill have been tortured, pitied, scorned, feared, laughed at, and denigrated, but not always cured.

There has been and still is, a stigma attached to psychological problems. According to the new college edition of the *American Heritage Dictionary of the English Language,* published in 1979, the archaic meaning of stigma is ''a mark burned into the skin of a criminal or slave; a brand.'' The medical meaning of stigma is ''a mark indicative of a history of a disease or abnormality,'' and the Greek meaning is ''a tattoo mark.'' The modern general meaning of stigma is ''a mark or token of infamy, disgrace, or reproach.'' To some extent and in some manner all of these meanings of stigma aptly reflect and characterize the current attitude toward mental illness. Even today, in some cases, having an emotional illness is a cause for disgrace and a basis for reproach. The discrimination and prejudice, however, are often more subtle.

Three basic threads of thought about mental illness have permeated civilization from earliest times. Attempts have been made to explain behavior disorders in physical or organic terms, namely, the somatogenic hypothesis; attempts have been made at psychological explanations, namely, the psychogenic hypothesis; and finally attempts have been made at magical explanations of mental disturbances.

The magical approach is related to using supernatural explanations as a basis for understanding the unknown. Primitive man believed that abnormal behavior was due to some outside power, like an evil spirit, which had taken possession of the victim. Note, also, that primitive man believed that physical illness was also caused by the spiritual forces of evil. The Greek poet Homer, writing about the eighth or seventh century B.C. proposed that persons suffering from insanity must have angered the gods, who punished them by causing them to behave irrationally. Therefore when Ulysses had a mental breakdown he plowed sand instead of fields, and when Ajax became deranged he killed sheep instead of his enemies. In the Stone Age trephining was a crude surgical procedure used to treat mental illness. During these early periods of time holes were chipped in the skulls of the unfortunates who had emotional problems to permit the evil spirits to escape. It was assumed that these evil spirits were causing aberrant behavior. At one time it was also believed that an evil being (semiautonomous), such as the devil, could reside within a person and take control of the body and mind. This is called demonology.

Thousands of years after the Stone Age the ancient Hebrews believed that behavior was controlled by good or bad spirits that had taken possession of the individual. It is alleged that Jesus Christ "cured" a man with an "unclean spirit" by exorcising the devil from within him and casting it onto a herd of swine. According to the legend, the swine ran "violently down a steep place into the sea" because they were now possessed. Demonological belief was not unique to the early Christians and the Hebrews but also characterized the thinking of the ancient Chinese, Egyptians, and Greeks. These demons were treated by flogging and starvation and by more benign methods, such as ritual prayers, loud noises, and coercion of the person possessed to drink terrible-tasting brews. Deviant behavior was often treated with exorcism. The strong humanitarian concern of the Hebrews for people who were ill is reflected by a hospital in Jerusalem, primarily for the mentally ill, which existed as early as A.D. 490.

Hippocrates (460–370 B.C.), the father of modern medicine, although trained in exorcism often operated outside the ideology of his time. He challenged the Greek philosophy that the gods arbitrarily ordained the mental dispositions of individuals. Hippocrates suggested that mental illness had the same causes as any other illness and should therefore be treated as such. Deviant behavior was therefore due to brain pathology. Hippocrates accepted the somatogenic hypothesis about the behavior disorders. The treatments he suggested were different from exorcistic tortures. In treating depression, or melancholia as it was then called, Hippocrates suggested quietness, sobriety, sexual abstinence, and care in choosing food and drink. This treatment was supposedly healthy for the brain and the body. As pointed out in Chapter 2, Hippocrates believed that mental health was related to a delicate balance among four body humors, blood, black bile, yellow bile, and phlegm. An imbalance of the humors resulted in behavior disorders; for example, too much black bile produced melancholia, too much phlegm created sluggishness, too much yellow bile, irascibility, and too much blood, a changeable temperament. Although Hippocrates' theory of body humors and illness is not supported by scientific evidence, his fundamental proposition that human behavior is strongly influenced by body substances or structures and that mental illness is due to some imbalance or damage has relevance for today's theories of mental illness.

Historians have noted that when Galen, the Greek physician who had practiced in Rome, died in the third century A.D., the Dark Ages began for the treatment and study of mental illness. Galen, like Hippocrates before him, focused on the role of the brain in the etiology of abnormal behavior. After the death of Galen there were few advances in medicine and subsequently Roman physicians came to accept superstitious explanations, including demonology. With the advent of Christianity possession by evil spirits was an insult to God and the Church. Therefore the person who was mentally ill was doubly cursed—first by being ill and second by antagonizing the Church.

During the thirteenth century, toward the end of the Middle Ages, there were occasions of mass madness. *Tarantism,* a sort of possession by alien forces, started in Italy and spread throughout Europe. When bitten by a tarantula in the summer heat people ran out of their homes and danced around in a wild fashion. They were joined by others who had also been bitten by the spiders and by those who had been bitten in other summers. In some cases the consumption of alcoholic beverages was a factor that may have accounted for the manic behavior. Tarantism and other explosions of exuberant behavior in which mobs of people took part may have been a response to famine, social, political and religious oppression, and the disintegration of social institutions that characterized western Europe from the thirteenth to the sixteenth centuries.

Michel Foucault, the French psychologist and philosopher, has noted the relationship between attitudes toward mental illness and the disappearance of leprosy between 1200 and 1400. In the middle of the twelfth century there were 2000 houses for lepers in France and 220 in England and Scotland to accommodate a population of one and one-half million. As leprosy began to disappear, partly because of segregation, a vacuum was created and the negative attitudes directed toward the leper had to find another target. Mental illness was an obvious substitute, but it was not enough.

The enlightened people of the Renaissance (fourteenth to seventeenth centuries) invented a charming way of caring for their mad citizens. The mentally ill were put on a ship under the care of mariners, because evil and the sea attracted and deserved one another. "Ships of Fools" crossed back and forth across the seas and canals of Europe, carrying their captive cargoes of "crazies." For some of the mentally ill this traveling was like a vacation. Some enjoyed it, some got well, some withdrew even further, some deteriorated, and some died, isolated from their families. Every town, city, and village that had extruded its own lunatics could now enjoy the spectacle of ships full of the alien insane sailing into port. The seventeenth and eighteenth centuries were visited by a fair amount of economic depression and social unrest. To solve some of the problems created by these conditions the indigents were imprisoned with the criminals and were required to work. The mentally ill fitted quite "logically" between the socially maladjusted and the iniquitous.

During the Middle Ages the treatment of mental illness was the responsibility of the priests. These spiritual leaders prayed over the mentally ill and sprinkled them with holy water. But in their zeal to rid these unfortunates of the spirit of Satan they cursed both Satan and the patient. Eventually torture was substituted for prayer as a means of punishing the devil residing in the patient. Such was the aura of enlightenment that surrounded the treatment of the mentally ill.

Initially the religious establishment was aware of two types of possession by the devil, neither of which was beneficial to the possessed. In one type the victim was involuntarily seized by the devil as God's punishment for sins committed. This was a personal misfortune. In the other, individuals intentionally entered into a contract with the devil and became witches with supernatural powers, doing the devil's bidding. The witches could ruin crops, sicken cattle, strike down their enemies, ruin their community, influence the weather, make men impotent, and so on. At the beginning of the sixteenth century the distinction between these two forms of demoniacal possession became blurred. Many innocent people were labeled as witches or heretics, as causing floods and pestilence. When unexplainable events occurred, demoniacal possession was invoked to explain them and many unfortunate people were falsely accused. It was not only the man on the street who made these accusations. Noted leaders of the sixteenth century were also ready to point a finger; for example, one respected writer said "The greatest punishment God can afflict on the wicked . . . is to deliver them over to Satan. . . . I conclude it is merely the work of the devil." The man who penned these words was Martin Luther.

In 1484 Pope Innocent VIII issued a papal bull that instructed the clergy to be thorough in their search for witches throughout Europe. His proclamation was supported by Exodus XXII:18: "Thou shalt not suffer a witch to live." The spiritual, magical, and demoniacal explanations of mental illness originate in the bible. Deuteronomy VI:5 states: "The Lord will smite thee with madness." Though demons initiated madness, the ultimate responsibility and control resided with God. King Saul's depression, described in Book I of Samuel, was interpreted as being caused by an evil spirit sent by God. Saul attempted to persuade his servant to kill him, but when the servant refused the depressed monarch committed suicide (I Samuel XXXI:4). There are a number of biblical discussions and descriptions of epileptic fits and catatonic excitement. Nebuchadnezzar (605–562 B.C.), the king who rebuilt Babylon, thought he was a wolf and this delusion is dutifully described in the Bible.

Surprisingly enough, in medieval times the layman had a more enlightened attitude toward the mentally ill than the professional. In France, in the twelfth, thirteenth, and fourteenth centuries, the belief that psychosis was an emotional illness that could be cured by love and psychological means was recorded. In early medieval times the care of the insane, whether the madness was conceptualized as due to emotional factors or diabolic possession, was considered a community responsibility.

It was only during the fourteenth century that the insane were considered dangerous and became the targets of persecution. Paradoxically, the physical care of the mentally ill was better during the early

Middle Ages than in the seventeenth and eighteenth centuries. The Bethlehem Hospital in London, one of the first asylums for the insane, was initially quite different from the "hole" that was later called Bedlam. When Bethlehem Hospital opened the inmates were treated with compassion and concern. When they were well enough to leave the hospital under the supervision of their relatives they were provided with badges that would readmit them to the hospital if their illness recurred. The community provided them with so much sympathy and attention that frequently vagrants counterfeited the badges so that they might be considered ex-patients of Bethlehem. In the town of Gheel, Belgium, in the thirteenth century, there was an institution that took care of psychotic and retarded children. These children were frequently boarded out to and adopted by sympathetic and compassionate families in the neighborhood. Even the Franciscan monk Bartholomaeus Anglicus (c. 1480), who thought of insanity in demonological terms (angels and devils), still recommended rational therapy methods, including special diets, baths, and ointments.

Therefore not all was doom and gloom. Not every mental health institution was a "Snake Pit." Most of these isolated humane methods of treatment, in a sea of exorcism, were remnants from the past and were not original contributions of the Middle Ages. They were based on Greek tradition and reflected the Judeo-Christian spirit.

What was the justification for the witch hunts of the Middle Ages? During this time two Dominican monks, who also served as inquisitors in Northern Germany at the request of the Pope, put together the *Malleus Maleficarum* ("The Witches' Hammer"). This manual provided technical instructions for hunting witches and a rationale for these sporting activities. It proclaimed that witches were either stupid or heretics. It aso listed the various methods of detecting them. These cues or signs included red spots or areas of insensitivity on the skin, presumably made by the devil's claw which touched the victim to seal the pact of collusion between the devil and the possessed. The manual also gave instructions for examining and sentencing witches. At one time it was considered to be divinely inspired and was revered and respected by Catholics and Protestants alike. For 200 years hundreds of thousands of emotionally disturbed men, women, and children were tracked down, accused, and tortured. If they confessed and/or were found guilty, they were publicly executed by hanging, burning, or stoning. The manual provided the guidance, the procedures, and the justification.

Europe did not have a monopoly on witch hunting. In the 1600s it became a popular sport in the colonies of North America. In 1692 Salem, Massachusetts, became a hotbed for witch hunts. In the short period of a few months hundreds of persons were arrested, 19 were hanged, and one was even pressed to death. It is obvious that many of the persons accused of being possessed by the devil were mentally ill.

As mentioned earlier, there were islands of enlightenment in the seas of reactionary thought and behavior. One of these islands was Johann Weyer, a sixteenth-century German physician, who was born in 1515 in Grave, on the Meuse, in Holland. He believed that most "witches" were mentally or physically ill and that the monstrous acts inflicted on these poor individuals were unjust and unconscionable. Weyer is often regarded as the founder of modern psychiatry and was probably the first physician to specialize in mental illness. Weyer's major aim was to prove that witches were mentally ill and should therefore be treated by physicians rather than by the clergy. Weyer also empathized with the suffering of persecuted women. In 1550 Weyer became the private physician to Duke William of Julich, Berg, and Cleves, who was a chronic depressive and who had many relatives who had become insane. Because the Duke had noticed that witches showed many of the same symptoms as his relatives, he sympathized with Weyer's belief that these women were basically insane. In 1578 the Duke had a stroke and suffered periodic psychotic episodes. As a result he could no longer control the witch hunters in his duchies and Weyer was forced to leave his employment with the Duke, after working for him for 30 years. For the rest of his life Dr. Weyer held a position under the protection and jurisdiction of Countess Ann of Techlenburg. It is poetic justice that Weyer, who was a crusader in defending women against witch hunters, was himself protected and saved by a woman.

Johann Weyer visited the domains of the Duke, especially Julich and Berg, to examine all alleged cases of witchcraft. He carefully collected data and interviewed both the accusers and victims. Weyer then systematically and carefully exposed the accusations and provided naturalistic explanations for the bizarre and deviant behavior. His meticulous case studies provide definite psychiatric descriptions of various mental illnesses. Weyer investigated the absurdities of witch-

1800 a fair number of physicians had carefully reported and classified their observations, but even the attempts at psychiatric classification by such skilled clinicians as Philippe Pinel (1745–1826) and Vincenzo Chiarugi (1759–1820) led to a general nosology but no basic understanding of emotional discomfort. When there is no psychological understanding of mental illness the mere observation of psychiatric patients, no matter how careful and how astute, results in classification but isn't much help. A classification of various phenomena does not explain them.

Classification can become rigidified and ossified and an end in itself. People develop vested interests in classification schemes and factual data that do not fit the scheme are ignored. Therefore the classification scheme may contain many errors and may be influenced by political and social factors. This was true of the earliest attempts. To some extent, I am sorry to say, this is also true of the DSM-III classification scheme of 1980. The methods of treatment of the mentally ill at the end of the eighteenth century were hardly affected by the classification schemes in existence at that time. Combinations of primitive physiological and psychological methods, based on speculation, continued to be used.

The best known eighteenth century proponent of a classification scheme, based on speculation, was the Dutch physician Hermann Boerhaave (1668–1738) of Leiden. Boerhaave was stongly influenced by Hipporates and accepted the now discredited notion of the relationship between illness and the four body humors. To Boerhaave melancholia was an illness caused by an excess of black bile, and his students spread this doctrine throughout Europe. Psychotherapy which involved bloodletting and purgatives, dousing the sick in ice-cold water, or some method putting the patient in a state of near shock.

Boerhaave developed one of the first shock instruments, a gyrating chair that rendered the recipient unconscious. Benjamin Rush (1745–1813), founder of psychiatry in the United States, used this gyrating chair on his patients, because he contended that congested blood in the brain caused mental illness and that the disorder would be cured by a rotary movement. Erasmus Darwin (1731–1802), a physician and Charles Darwin's grandfather, postulated that all illnesses were due to "disordered motions" of the nervous tissues of the body. He believed that the rotating chair would set everything straight.

During the eighteenth century physicians in general were concerned with the exotic, unusual, bizarre, and extraordinary features of the behavior disorders. Some students of Boerhaave did become interested in the symptoms of neurotics and proposed classification schemes, albeit different ones, of mental illness based on physiology. George Cheyne (1671–1743), for example, suggested that neurotic behavior was common in England and pointed out that he himself, a Fellow of the College of Physicians at Edinburgh, was neurotic. He noted that anyone could suffer from emotional problems and that there was no need to be humiliated by it. His book, published in 1733, was entitled *The English Malady: or a Treatise of nervous diseases of all kinds, as spleen, vapours, lowness of spirits, hypochondriacal and distempers.* His classification scheme was based on Hippocrates' theory of humors. It substituted classification for explanation.

Robert Whytt (1714–1766) divided the neuroses into hysteria, hypochondriasis, and nervous exhaustion ("neurasthenia") and theorized that disturbed movements within the nervous system produced nervous problems. (Note that this is not too different in principle from some current biochemical models of nervous disorders.) Probably the most comprehensive classification scheme of mental illness was proposed by William Cullen (1712–1790). Philippe Pinel was so impressed by Cullen's scheme that he incorporated it into his own classification.

Cullen used the methods of Carolus Linnaeus (1707–1778), Swedish botanist and physician, who classified plants and animals, and François Bossier de Sauvages (1706–1767), a physician who described and organized 2000 diseases into classes, orders, and genera. De Sauvages' eighth class, the *folies*, was a detailed, comprehensive, and systematic description of every facet of nervous illness. Cullen, who was at Edinburgh, was the first to use the term "neurosis" to refer to illnesses that are not related to local pathology or fever (temperature). He had a fourfold classification of the neuroses: Comata (apoplexy, stroke); Adynamiae (changes in the autononic nervous system); Spasmi (disturbances of voluntary muscles, e.g., convulsions), and Vesaniae (intellectual impairment). Cullen postulated that neurosis was due to a decay of the intellect or of the voluntary or involuntary nervous system. Neurotic illnesses and the various symptoms were due to physiological breakdowns—not to demons!

Cullen postulated a physiological basis for melancholia:

It may be observed that in it (melancholia) there is a degree of torpor in the motion of the nervous power both with respect to sensation and volition, and there is a general rigidity of the simple solids, and that the balance of the sanguiferous system is upon the side of the veins.

Cullen's therapeutic approaches were exercise, physiotherapy, diet, cold dousings, blistering of the forehead, purging, bloodletting, and vomiting—the standard and typical methods of treating physiological illnesses at that time. When it came to seriously disturbed patients Cullen used the methods of his colleagues: threats, severe restraint, and straitjackets.

Giovanni Battista Morgagni, an Italian physician from the University of Padua, investigated 800 autopsies in detail over a half century and in 1761 published one of the most significant and remarkable medical documents of all time: *De sedibus et causis moborum per anatomen indagatis* ("On the Seats and Causes of Disease Investigated by Anatomy"). Morgagni believed that illnesses were related to specific organs. In his studies he focused on brain pathology. He discovered that the symptoms caused by a stroke were not due to brain pathology per se but rather to broken blood vessels that affected the brain. He was also the first to observe and report that the paralysis that appeared after a stroke was on the side of the body that was opposite to the areas of the brain hemorrhage. As a result of Morgagni's work, many neurologists, neuroanatomists, and physicians interested in mental illness attempted to localize these diseases in the brain, although without too much success. Concomitant with this switch from useless Hippocratic physiology to cerebral localization, there were changes in mental asylums in the direction of more humanitarianism. Many of the madhouses became hospitals and this facilitated humane and effective treatment.

The takeover of treatment of mental illness by the medical establishment did not lead automatically to more effective and humane therapeutic techniques. Benjamin Rush (1745–1813) was positive that mental illness was due to an excess of blood in the brain. Therefore he drew great quantities of blood, even up to six quarts over a period of a few months. It should be noted that his patients became less agitated. Of course! All their strength was gone. Rush also believed that many "insane people" could be cured if you really frightened them. One technique was to convince the patient that death was imminent. This was done by placing the patient in a coffinlike box, pierced with holes and lowering the box into a tank of water. The patient was kept under water until the bubbles of air stopped rising, after which the patient was taken out, rubbed, and revived.

Philippe Pinel (1745–1826), physician, teacher, philosopher, and reformer, also proposed a classification system of behavior disorders late in the eighteenth century. He was physician-in-chief at Bicêtre and La Salpêtrière and knew many of the politicians and intellectuals in the troubled times of the French Revolution. On the basis of observations made on his hospital patients, Pinel developed a simple and practical classification scheme for mental illness. He categorized the psychoses into melancholias, manias without delirium, manias with delirium, and dementia (idiocy and intellectual deterioration). His descriptions of symptoms were systematic and superb. He differentiated among problems of attention, memory, and judgment and recognized the importance of the emotions in mental illness. Pinel thought that mental disorders might possibly be due to a lesion in the central nervous system because he believed that physical factors caused behavior disorders. For Pinel, mental illness was a natural phenomenon and the result of heredity and life events, including emotional experience. Observation and systematic classification of symptoms were important techniques in his repertory. Pinel took a psychological orientation and, in addition to being influenced by rational inquiry, was also concerned with social reform, especially of the asylums.

Even though the mentally ill had not been tortured at the stake for some time, their situation during the Enlightenment, the eighteenth century, was not exactly characterized by days of wine and roses. Those who were not hospitalized often wandered aimlessly through the countryside and were ridiculed, scorned, and sometimes beaten. During the medieval period Bethlehem Hospital in England treated psychotics humanely and kindly. In the eighteenth century, however, this was not the case. Bethlehem (or Bedlam as it came to be known, and which became a word in the English language that stands for chaos, confusion, or wild uproar) became a favorite Sunday outing place for Londoners who came to gawk at the madmen through the iron gates. According to Michel Foucault, even as late as 1815 the hospital at Bethlehem exhibited lunatics to the public for a penny every Sunday. The annual revenue for these "shows" was about 400 British pounds, which means there were about 96,000 visits a year. Until the French Revolution trips to the Bicêtre and the exhibition of the insane was also a popular Sunday outing for the Left Bank bourgeoisie of Paris. Anyone could visit the Bicêtre, and on a nice sunny day at least 2000 persons paid their money for a guided tour. Certain attendants, by flicking their whips, were specialists at making the mad dance and do acrobatics. By the end of the eighteenth century the mad were exhibiting the mad.

During the Enlightenment Bethlehem was certainly Bedlam. The conditions were filthy, the food was abominable, the darkness and isolation were terrifying, and the treatment by the attendants was brutal. Therapy consisted of emetics, purgatives, bloodletting, and "harmless" tortures provided by special paraphernalia. The general conditions at the Bicêtre, which became part of the General Hospital in 1660 and held "madmen," and at the La Salpêtrière, which held "madwomen", in chains, were definitely no better than those at "Bedlam." In the "Lunatics' Tower" in Vienna, built in 1784, the inmates were located in the spaces between the outer and the inner walls. From that vantage point they could be observed from below by people passing by. The Pennsylvania Hospital in Philadelphia, St. Luke's Hospital in England, the Hospital for the Insane in Moscow, and the Narrenthurm in Vienna provided room and board and segregation and were considered havens of respite compared with Bethlehem during the second half of the eighteenth century. In Paris, London, and New York the police had the same code, which was that when a dangerous person who was mad had no relatives that person was jailed. This was not necessarily bad because prison conditions were about the same as those in the mental hospitals, and in jail at least the inmate was not brutalized, physically or mentally.

Jean Baptiste Pussin "the governor of the insane," first at Bicêtre and then at La Salpêtrière, in conjunction with Philippe Pinel, released the patients from their chains, opened their windows, provided them with nourishing food, treated them with tender loving care, and initiated other reforms. This was at the height of the French Revolution in the 1790s. (Pinel took over as head of the Bicêtre in 1793 and two years later at La Salpêtrière. Pussin, a lay administrator, was associated with Pinel at both hospitals and probably initiated many of the reforms credited to Pinel). It is little known, but in contrast to the cruel methods of treating the insane in England and France, there were more humane traditions, especially in Spain. It is likely that the physicians in Valencia in 1405, rather than Pussin and Pinel, were the first to remove the chains and to initiate a more humane form of treatment. Diet, hygiene, entertainment, games, and free exercise were part of the treatment in Valencia. Agricultural work was part of the treatment in the Saragossa asylum. This was probably the first form of occupational therapy. In 1792 William Tuke of England founded the York Retreat, a benevolent, comfortable haven for the mentally ill.

Why were mental patients treated so harshly during the Enlightenment of the eighteenth century? There are a number of reasons. First, there was almost complete ignorance of the nature of mental illness. Although progress was being made toward an understanding of physical illness, no such progress was being made toward mental illness. No one saw black humors, no one observed the movements of "animal spirits," and no one discovered any physiological locus for emotional disturbance. A second factor was that it was then believed that mental illness was incurable. This frustrated therapists and made it difficult to be nice to the patients. A third factor was the dread or fear of the insane; that is a fear of the unknown and the deviant. We tend to ostracize and reject and are hostile toward those who are different.

(Much of the material of a historical nature I have learned by reading *The History of Psychiatry*, an excellent book by Franz G. Alexander and Sheldon T. Selesnick, published by Harper and Row in 1966. Unfortunately, this book and the paperback version published in 1968 by Mentor are out of print.)

As pointed out in Chapter 2, there have been three major advances in the treatment of mental illness, especially depression. The first was due to Pinel and Pussin in the 1790s, the second to Freud, about 1900, and the third to the biochemical revolution of the 1950s. Despite these advances, a stigma is still attached to the mentally ill. The reason I have spent so much time discussing the historical aspects of attitudes toward mental illness is to provide a context for understanding today's attitudes and to demonstrate that negative attitudes are not new with our generation, with our era. Things have been much worse! Of course, things could be better.

We pride ourselves in Western Civilization in being rational human beings, but mental illness is not a rational phenomenon. It is an irrational, emotional expression of biochemical, constitutional, genetic, and psychological factors. Because we attempt to understand things rationally, the apparent irrational nature of mental illness symptoms frustrates us. Most important, however, we fear the unknown and reject the deviant. Studies in social psychology have shown that the deviant is treated like an outcast. When someone is ill, be it physical or mental, it is an aberration from the norm and it makes us uncomfortable. I still recall vividly when I was six years old and had the mumps. After a week or so, when I had recuperated, I returned to the street to play with the gang. One of my "friends" said to the others, "Don't play with him, he's been sick." I ran home crying, feeling utterly forlorn. With mental illness these attitudes are compounded by the fact that we, the public, can't cope with it. Furthermore, someone else's illness attests to our own vulnerability and mortality and makes us ashamed. One day we may encounter a friend who is well and functioning properly; the next day that friend may be depressed. . . . "There but for the grace of God go I." Because all of us at one time during our lives will know at least one person with a depression or other emotional illness, it is important that we examine our own attitudes and those of our friends and relatives toward mental illness.

Depression has received a fair amount of publicity. The bias of society toward depressed patients became manifest during the 1972 presidential campaign in the United States. Senator George McGovern, the presidential nominee of the Democratic Party, proposed Senator Thomas Eagleton as his vice-presendential running mate. Eagleton had once been treated for depression; part of his treatment consisted of ECT. For some reason, either because he was concerned about societal stigma or because he saw the treatment as a private concern, Eagleton did not tell McGovern about his depression. If Eagleton had been concerned that he would be stigmatized and deprived of the nomination if his treatment for depression were publicly known, his fears were well founded. When the mass media learned about it, especially the ECT, McGovern dropped him from the ticket like a "hot potato." There was no doubt about Thomas Eagleton's competence. He has served and continues to serve effectively and excellently as a senator from Missouri. Biases die hard. Thomas Eagleton was stigmatized for having been depressed. This was in 1972. Do these biases and this stigma attached to depression still exist?

Reactions to my Depression

What were some of the reactions of my colleagues, friends, family, and doctors toward my depression? I have alluded to some of these attitudes in earlier chapters. At this point, I should like to integrate and systematize some of my impressions of the reactions of others toward me before, during, and after my depression. I also discuss some of my own attitudes.

In April 1977, when I first started getting depressed, not only did I deny it to myself but so did my friends and colleagues. My secretary and administrative assistant, as indicated earlier, asked me what was wrong. My gradual withdrawal from interaction, my lack of cheerfulness, and my quietness were interpreted by them as anger at something done wrong. After about four weeks my wife insisted that I should see a doctor. My children said nothing to me. My colleagues at York said nothing to me, and the professionals (psychiatrists, psychologists, and social workers) in the Department of Psychiatry, Toronto East General Hospital, said nothing to me. I'm sure that some, if not most of them, must have noticed that something was wrong with me. (If they had not, they shouldn't be working in the mental health field.)

Why did my colleagues participate in an unintended "conspiracy of silence"? There are a number of factors to consider. First, suppose they commented on my depression and they were wrong. Suppose I wasn't really depressed but only very tired. This would have been most embarrassing for them. Second, some people do not like to interfere or intrude in the lives of others. Third, suppose it were true that I was depressed. How could they handle it without embarrassing me? The fact that I was chairman might have been another factor. Because the "show" was running smoothly, there was no need to question the chief executive officer. My guess is that my friends didn't say anything because they probably couldn't believe that it was true. I have an even temperament and am quite happy-go-lucky. Being depressed is dissonant with my usual demeanor. Therefore my friends probably ignored the overt cues that indicated the onset of my depression. I should, however, point out that a few of them, on occasion, did say to me "Are you OK, Norm? You look tired." When I said I was fine, they did not press it, but they may have discussed it among themselves. In this they were following a social norm or social convention of not intruding into the personal life of another. Furthermore, when I was hypomanic, none of my colleagues or friends confronted me. Here, again, they were following the social norm of not interfering. Because I had previously been depressed, they probably perceived it as a recuperative period and gave me the benefit of the doubt. How does one handle such a situation? Should they have interfered and taken the possible risk of embarrassing themselves and me? Although it is a difficult thing to do, there are at least two approaches one can take. If a number of colleagues and friends were concerned about me, they might have confronted me jointly. If this didn't get anywhere, they could have voiced their concerns to my wife. But conventions die hard and we are leery of intruding into the private lives of others.

One of the biggest surprises occurred when I went to see my GP. As I indicated in Chapter 3, when I saw him on June 2, 1977, and told him that I was depressed, he insisted that I see a psychiatrist in Oshawa, which is more than 30 miles east of Toronto. He was concerned for my welfare. He was worried that I might be exposed if I saw someone in Toronto. Surely, if I had asked him about my gall bladder or my appendix he wouldn't have had the same concern. I was doubly surprised because my GP is psychologically sophistcated. He is an excellent diagnostician and does some psychotherapy himself. Yet, probably without being consciously aware of it he was worried about my consulting someone in Toronto. Somehow there is still a stigma attached to seeing a psychiatrist. It isn't something one discusses publicly. If physicians, and even psychiatrists, have difficulty in accepting the fact that there is nothing wrong in seeing a psychiatrist, how can we expect the public to have a more benign and accepting attitude? Old attitudes die hard. There is still an important educational task ahead.

With respect to negative attitudes about mental health, I was not exactly blameless myself. Why did I wait to see a doctor from April 1977, when the first symptoms of my depression appeared, until the beginning of June, when I just about collapsed? Was it because I thought I could handle it myself as a psychologist? Or was it, perhaps, by admitting that I was having an emotional problem I was also admitting my human frailty and weakness? Perhaps, unconsciously I felt that there was a stigma attached to seeing someone about one's emotional problems. Because I am a clinical psychologist, this would be somewhat ironic. I don't really know for sure, but I do know that if I had a physical ailment that persisted for so long I would have seen a doctor much sooner. Old attitudes die hard! I do, however, know that the second time I became depressed, in April 1978, I immediately sought help. I had learned my lesson well.

I have already mentioned my fears and biases about hospitalization and my initial biases against ECT. It should be noted that although most psychiatrists proclaim that ECT is the treatment of choice for depression they do not use it until they have tried the antidepressants. I think that there are several reasons for this. One is that it is simpler to prescribe drugs than to administer ECT. Drugs do not involve the use of hospital facilities, whereas ECT, even if administered on an outpatient basis, involves hospital facilities and also the use of more personnel. I believe, however, that the major reason for preferring drugs to ECT as an initial course of treatment is that psychiatrists are concerned about the prejudices and biases that the public has toward ECT. The public still stigmatizes ECT and psychiatrists do not want to be hassled. Perhaps some of this "stigma" rubs off on them.

There are social class factors involved in terms of who receives ECT and its effectiveness. According to Dr. Leonard Cammer, a psychiatrist, lower and/or lower middle class individuals often seem to recover from depression more readily than upper middle class or upper class persons. In general, the lower and lower middle class patient has a less negative attitude toward ECT and accepts it more readily as a course of treatment. The lower class and middle class person cannot afford a long-term illness. I was able to enjoy the "luxury" of being ill the whole summer of 1977 and did not suffer financially because of it. ECT was not tried on me until after three months. During my second depression, when I had to be in good shape for my trip to Oxford, ECT was administered almost immediately. The lower and lower middle class person is strongly motivated to find the treatment that will work most rapidly and effectively and that will get him or her back to work as quickly as possible. The lower class person would be more likely to accept an inpatient course of ECT treatment, whereas most middle class and upper middle class persons would prefer ECT on an outpatient basis.

The upper classes, especially the intellectuals, would also be more concerned about mental "impairment." They would be concerned about memory loss due to ECT. What most people don't realize is that the depression itself "fogs up" a person's mental and perceptual abilities. Most of the time the effects of depression on memory are secondary. Depression dulls our perceptions and we can neither concentrate nor pay attention. In many cases we fail to perceive aspects of the world about us. If we don't see things, we can't remember them. Therefore it is important to point out to a depressed person that he or she will not function effectively or on an adequate intellectual basis until the depression lifts. Because of this, effective treatment should commence immediately, be it ECT or drugs.

There is a general relationship between social class and mental illness. The lower classes are more likely to suffer from mental illness (except for the neuroses) than the upper classes. Lower class people are more likely to be hospitalized for depression and schizophrenia than the upper classes. This may be due in part to the harsher environmental experiences that the lower classes encounter, to a greater extent of family disorganization, or to the unlikelihood of their having access to private psychiatric care. Perhaps we are more likely to protect the upper classes from hospitalization. As I noted earlier in Chapter 5, Dr. Persad had mentioned that if I needed hospitalization they would not admit me to the Clarke Institute but instead would send me to Homewood, which is 50 miles from Toronto. The concern was that I was too well known in Toronto and especially at the Clarke Institute and would less likely to be known at Homewood. In fact, one psychiatrist suggested that I use a pseudonym. Dr. Persad wanted to protect me from being recognized and perhaps embarrassed. Did he see any stigma in being hospitalized? In all fairness to Dr. Persad, he knew of my morbid fear of hospitals and probably felt that if the need arose I would feel less uncomfortable outside Toronto. This, however, would have meant losing Dr. Persad as a therapist, a trade off I was not ready to make. But, this is all academic now because I didn't require hospitalization.

Probably the thing that most surprised me was the attitude of some psychiatrists toward my going public. I received, as indicated earlier, such comments as "this shows poor judgment on your part Norm"; or "this will ruin your career, Norm." If I had wanted to write about my gall bladder operation, I'm sure I should not have received such reactions. When Norman Cousins wrote about his recovery from a crippling and supposedly irreversible physical illness in his book

Anatomy of an Illness I'm certain that no one told him that his career would be ruined. Could it be that some psychiatrists were projecting their own feelings? The attitudes of society rub off on all of us. Psychiatrists are part of society and despite their professional training are not completely immune to these attitudes. I must add that other psychiatrists have been most encouraging. They felt that my going public would help others who were depressed and would also, to some extent, help to counteract the attitude that there is a stigma attached to depression.

Experiences such as mine, when made public, can have the effect of educating the public. It helps depressed people to know that they are not alone in their afflictions, that the affective disorders are a common malaise. Books such as this one can help to clear the air. Clifford Beers, a graduate of Yale, had experienced a number of psychotic episodes for which he was treated in three mental hospitals. When he recovered he wrote a book entitled *The Mind that Found Itself* (1908), wherein he describes being restrained in a straitjacket and the emotional problems created by the terrible custodial care. This book, which has gone through about eight editions since 1908, led to the creation of the mental-hygiene movement and helped to promote better care for the mentally ill. It led to consciousness raising with respect to the treatment and attitudes about emotional problems. Beers himself devoted the rest of his life to improving the lot of patients in mental hospitals.

Lest I be accused of being too harsh in my criticisms of the attitudes of psychiatrists toward mental health, let me point out that some of my psychologist colleagues have fared no better. I have already mentioned the professional immaturity of some who tried to interfere with my course of ECT treatment or told me not to bother to take my medication. What surprised me most were those who came or did not come to visit me. Certainly all my close friends did and many people became close friends as a result of my illness. My family and I found their support most helpful. During the course of my illness one of the few things I felt good about was the opportunity to interact with other people.

Why did some people neither visit nor phone me? My guess is that many of them felt uncomfortable about the whole thing. For some of them it might have hit too close to home—a sort of ''There but for the grace of God go I'' reaction. Perhaps some of my colleagues can handle mental illness in a professional patient-doctor relationship but not on a collegial level. Some may have been away for the summer; others may have been busy, although this is a flimsy excuse; and some might just not have cared. Nevertheless, I found it then and still find it now a rather puzzling situation.

The group that had the least bias about my illness and attached the least stigma to it was the one that had the most vested interest in it; namely, my family. As I have indicated earlier, my family was extremely supportive and I do not know how I would have survived without them. In fact, without my family it probably would have been necessary to hospitalize me. My guess is that many depressed people are hospitalized because of their lack of family support rather than because of the severity of their illness. There are a lot of stresses and strains on the fabric of the family. The person for whom my illness created the most difficult was probably my wife. I could lie around feeling sorry for myself but she had to pick up the pieces. Neither my wife nor my children complained about my illness. None of them attached any stigma to it. They accepted it and tried to make the best of a difficult situation. They did this with grace, charm, and courage and sometimes even with humor. For this I am eternally grateful. In many ways I believe we are a stronger family unit because of my illness. Adversity brought us closer together. I was not treated as an outcast by my family but as a valuable and valued member. Someone could say, well they had no choice. Yes, they had. I'm certain that if my wife had told Dr. Persad that she couldn't cope with the situation he would have had me hospitalized. My family, especially my wife, were high on courage and low on bias and prejudice with respect to my depression.

One of the other things that I found most gratifying was the attitude of people toward me after I had recovered. I was not treated as an invalid; I was not treated with "kid gloves"; I was not treated as a "nut" or a "weirdo." I was treated as a valued colleague and a good friend. In short, my friends and colleagues did not change their attitude toward me because I had been ill. They reacted to me as they had done in the past, which is exactly the way I wanted them to react. I mentioned this to Tom Schofield. Tom said he was not surprised:

> People usually go by your track record. Norm, you're doing everything you did before and just as competently. You are living up to their expectations of you. You did things well before and you're doing them well now. That's why their attitudes are positive toward you.

12
Where Do We Go from Here?

Where do we go from here? What have I learned from my depression, or, more correctly, my bipolar affective disorder, and where am I at now? Can what I have learned be helpful to others and if so, how? This is a heady set of questions and obviously any answers will be filtered through my own personality and attitudes. I am hopeful that this will serve as a prism that refracts light rather than one that distorts it.

When I wrote the first draft of this chapter it was mid-April, 1980—April 15 or Income Tax Day in the United States, when everyone pays their dues. It is now April 1981, four years since I suffered my first depression in 1977. I am feeling fine now. I am neither depressed nor hypomanic. I spent my sabbatical leave in the Psychology Department at Stanford University and lived in Palo Alto. In addition to writing this book, I worked on a personality textbook and an invited chapter for an edited book on consistency and variability of behavior. While at Stanford I attended some seminars and presented some talks in the area and in my opinion functioned at a normal level. I lived in Palo Alto, without my family, from the end of October until the end of April, when I returned to Toronto.

Although I feel like my old self now, I did not feel that way when I started recovering from my second depression in the summer of 1978. Although my first depression lifted with a "bang" after the ECT in September 1977, the second depression lifted imperceptibly with a "whimper", starting in July 1978. About the middle of that month I began to feel a bit better and even drove the car occasionally. As indicated earlier, Dr. Persad was concerned that I might be getting a little high and started me on a course of lithium treatment. During

154

August I resumed most of my activities, including those related to the chairmanship. Initially I had some hand tremors as side effects of the lithium, but once the lithium treatment was stabilized the tremors disappeared. The anxiety and the depression disappeared by the end of August, but I still felt restrained. I did not feel like my old self. In many ways I was subdued and felt as if I were on a leash. This was probably due to the lithium. The fine tuning of the lithium was slowing down my "level of idling." My wife stated that in her opinion I was the same as I had always been except that I had lost some of my ebullience.

By the spring of 1979, however, I was back to my old self. My ebullience had returned. I was my old effervescent self again. The medication I was taking consisted of 600 mg of lithium (two capsules) and 150 mg of Elavil a day. I saw Dr. Persad once a month, except during April when I saw him twice. April came and went without any problems. I did not get depressed. The crisis month had passed uneventfully.

In June 1979 I went to Stockholm to participate in an International Symposium on the "The Situation in Psychological Theory and Research." This symposium was organized by my good friend and colleague David Magnusson, and was being held on the island of Lidingö, a suburb of Stockholm. I arrived a few days before the conference and stayed at David's house. During 1973–1974, my previous sabbatical, my family and I had lived in Stockholm and I collaborated closely with David, who at that time was the Chairman of the Psychology Department at the University of Stockholm. David had visited me in Toronto in December 1974, and my family and I had returned to Stockholm in June 1975, when David and I organized an International Symposium on Interactional Psychology. David and I have coedited two books and have written a number of journal articles. When David found out in the summer of 1977 that I was depressed, he was extremely upset. He was also quite disturbed when he visited me in Toronto in April 1978 and discovered that I had had another attack of depression. Therefore David was especially pleased to see me in June 1979 at his home in Lidingö and to note that I was healthy again. I was very pleased to see David and to discuss old times and our continued collaborative writing on interactional psychology.

The Stockholm symposium (held at Lovik) went very well and I saw many old friends and made new ones. It was especially pleasing to see

Holiday of Darkness

Michael Argyle from Oxford and J. McVicker Hunt, who had been my
Ph.D. dissertation advisor at the University of Illinois. Joe Hunt and I
have collaborated on research on anxiety ever since I had finished my
dissertation. In 1944 Joe edited a handbook on *Personality and the
Behavior Disorders* which has since become a classic in the field. Joe
had asked me to collaborate with him on the revision of *Personality and
the Behavior Disorders* (affectionately known as P and BD) and during
the symposium at Lovik he and I met to discuss the revision. One of the
projects I worked on during my sabbatical at Stanford is the revision of
P and BD.

After the symposium I went to London with one of my colleagues
from the conference. We saw some plays and the sights and after a few
days I took the train up to Oxford to visit Michael Argyle. Michael and
two of his students were planning a conference and a subsequent book
on the psychological study of situations. Although I later declined to
attend the conference at Oxford in November (I had to be at Stanford
then) I did agree to write a chapter for their book. I returned to Toronto
toward the end of June, ready to celebrate my twenty-fourth wedding
anniversary, and looking forward to completing my term as chairman
and to moving out of the chairman's office.

My successor as chairman asked me to stay on until the middle of
July because he was planning to take a vacation. I agreed to do so
because there was not much going on during the summer and these extra
two weeks would allow me to move my material from the chairman's
office into my regular faculty office at a leisurely pace. (It would also
allow me to throw out stuff I didn't really need.) At the beginning of
July my wife and I visited her sister and brother-in-law for a long
weekend in Ottawa. It was relaxing and enjoyable. We went to a play,
took walks, and played tennis. I had finished much of the move into my
faculty office before we went to Ottawa. It was a relief not being
chairman any more and to my pleasant surprise I didn't miss it. The
transition was much smoother than expected. I was looking forward to
my sabbatical which began officially on July 1.

During the last week of July my wife and I flew to Vancouver for a
one-week vacation. This was probably the first summer vacation that
we had taken without our children. My son was working during the
summer and as part of his work visited Calgary, Edmonton, Banff,
Quebec City, and Montreal. My daughter was planning to go on

vacation to Vancouver and Calgary, with a girl friend, in mid-August. Beatty and I had a leisurely holiday. We saw the sights in Vancouver, took a boat to Nanaimo on Vancouver Island, the train to Victoria, and a boat back to Vancouver. The weather was gorgeous and we did a lot of walking and sightseeing. We returned at the beginning of August, and I was prepared to complete the writing of my chapter for an edited handbook on "Stress and Anxiety." I had promised the editors that I would have it completed before the end of August.

We returned from Vancouver early Thursday morning, August 2, 1979. I played tennis on Friday afternoon and on Saturday my wife and I went downtown for a relaxing day. We stayed home that evening, but before we went to bed I ate about half a jar of peanuts. My wife went to sleep. When I got into bed I felt a pressure, not a pain, in my chest, around the sternum, because of which it took me about an hour or so, much longer than usual, to fall asleep. When I awoke Sunday morning the pressure was gone. Some friends, a couple from Ottawa, were coming over for lunch and after lunch I was to play tennis with the husband. During lunch the pressure reappeared but I ignored it and didn't mention it to anyone. I went to play tennis, with the temperature in the high 80s (Fahrenheit). The only effect the chest pressure had on my tennis game was to slow me down. I returned home and our friends from Ottawa left. By late afternoon my wife asked me if I would go to the airport to pick up our son who was returning from Calgary. I told her about the pressure in my chest. She decided to go for our son herself and remarked that if the pressure hadn't disappeared by the time she returned she would take me to the emergency ward of the hospital.

When my wife and son returned from the airport she asked me how I felt. I told her that the chest pressure hadn't disappeared but that I wanted dinner before we went to the hospital. She refused to make dinner and insisted that we go to the hospital first. She won! When we arrived at the hospital and I told them what the problem was they took me into the emergency ward and told me to get undressed and lie on a bed. They took my pulse, blood pressure, temperature, and some blood tests. They were astonished that my blood pressure was 200/110. This was dangerously high. Other than the reaction to Parnate, I had never had a high blood pressure. The doctor ordered an electrocardiagram (EKG).

Finally, the duty doctor, who fortunately happened to be the head of internal medicine, examined me. He asked me if I ever had an EKG and if I remembered anything about it. I informed him that my GP had taken one a few years ago and that Dr. Persad had arranged for me to have one before the ECT. In both cases, to the best of my knowledge, the EKG was normal. The doctor told me that the present EKG showed some slight irregularities, that the blood tests showed some enzyme changes, and all this coupled with the high blood pressure and the pressure in my chest suggested the possibility of a mild heart attack. Therefore he suggested that I stay in the hospital overnight. Beatty, who was there at the time, almost had a heart attack herself. I treated it very calmly and asked to have some supper. My reaction might have been due to the calm, soothing, and psychologically sophisticated way in which the doctor broke the news to us, to denial on my part, or to a combination of the two.

In any case, they took me to the intensive care unit, gave me some toast and tea, gave me my Elavil, and arranged for me to have lithium and Elavil the next day. They offered me a sleeping pill which I declined. They then hooked me up for continuous EKG monitoring. The next morning, when I awoke, the chest pressure was gone and it has never reappeared, at least as of now. The next day a cardiac specialist came to examine me. The chief internist and the cardiologist, after examining me Monday morning, both concluded that I had probably had a mild heart attack (myocardial infarction or infarct) and that I would have to remain in the hospital for about two weeks. Because I felt perfectly fine by this time, I thought all of this was silly, but I didn't plan to press my luck. I remained in intensive care for about two or three days and was then placed in a regular ward for about six days and finally in a self-care unit ward where patients get dressed and eat in a common dining room. I was in the hospital from Sunday August 5 until Tuesday August 21. I might add that the care was super. Many of my friends visited me, as, of course, did my wife and children, and I did a fair amount of reading.

Both Dr. Persad and my family doctor were away on vacation when I had my heart attack. My family doctor returned from his vacation after I had been in the hospital for about a week and I was put under his care after my discharge. Dr. Persad returned from his vacation a few days before I left the hospital. I saw Dr. Persad about a week later. Although the tricyclics do not cause heart attacks, Dr. Persad took me off the

Elavil, because once someone has had an infarct the tricyclics can cause complications. The suggestion is that these drugs should be used with extreme caution by persons with a history of myocardial infarction and/or congestive heart failure. Dr. Persad felt that the lithium would be sufficient to act as a prophylactic against the recurrence of my bipolar affective disorder. If hypomania recurred, it would be necessary to increase the dosage of lithium. If depression recurred, he would probably prescribe Ludiomil (maprotiline), which is a tetracyclic antidepressant, or Sinequan (doxepin), which is slightly different chemically from amitriptyline. Both produce fewer complications than amitriptyline for persons who have had cardiac problems. In any case, since the end of August 1979, I have not taken any antidepressants, and the only thing I have taken for my bipolar affective disorder is 600 mg of lithium a day. I have, however, been taking 120 mg of Inderal (40 mg three times a day) and a half tablet of Dyazide. The Inderal was reduced to 80 mg a day (two tablets) at the end of September 1980. If I remain symptom-free of my affective disorder until the fall of 1981, I will probably be taken off the lithium at that time.

The Inderal (propranolol) medication slows down the circulatory system, regulates the heart beat, and indirectly lowers blood pressure; it acts as a prophylaxis against angina pectoris. The Dyazide, an anti-hypertensive diurectic, lowers blood pressure. My blood pressure with this medication has been 130/80 or lower. My EKG is now fine and I feel in good health. The only slight complication is that both lithium and Inderal slow down the rate of metabolism. Therefore I have gained some weight which I have had difficulty losing. Otherwise, in terms of my affect and my physical health, I feel fine. I have been seeing my GP and Dr. Persad regularly.

My heart attack was on Sunday, August 5, 1979. (This is exactly eight years to the day that my father died. Those of you who are psychoanalytically inclined, please note.) Psychologically, my reaction to my heart attack was excellent. By the time I came to Stanford I had resumed all my normal activities, except for tennis, which I resumed after I had been at Stanford for about a week. I would have resumed this earlier if my GP had let me. My heart attack was much less upsetting to me than my depression.

As much as anything else, my reaction to my heart attack has convinced me that my bipolar affective disorder is biochemical rather than reactive. My reaction to my heart attack was one of benign acceptance. A heart attack is a serious thing, yet I treated it much less seriously than I had my depression. I was accused of reacting frivolously. Perhaps I was practicing the defense of denial. Perhaps I was thankful that it wasn't another depressive episode. I did not treat myself as an invalid, nor did I want to be treated that way. There are at least two general extreme reactions that one can have to a heart attack. At one extreme a person can behave like a invalid, be pampered, and refuse to resume all previous activities. On the other extreme, one can deny that a heart attack has occured and behave as if nothing had happened. Either extreme is dangerous.

Although I did tend in the direction of resuming all my activities as if nothing had happened, I did accept my heart attack and returned to my previous activities cautiously. I probably would have resumed them at a more rapid pace had not my GP and my wife restrained me. I was allowed to and encouraged to walk as much as possible. I wanted to start playing tennis again in September and to resume driving my car at the end of August. My family doctor did not permit me to drive until the end of September and I played tennis on November 9 in Palo Alto. When I came out of the hospital I saw my GP every week at first and then every two weeks until I left for Stanford. He has monitored my blood pressure and my EKG.

Psychologically, the heart attack has not left me with any scars. My reactions have been quite normal; in fact, supernormal. As I said earlier, unless I have been practicing extreme denial, I believe that my reaction has been a healthy one. I have taken a fatalistic approach. Nothing can be done about the heart attack I have had. However, there are certain things that I can do to cut down the probability of another. I do not smoke so that this is not a problem. However, I can make a valiant effort to lose weight by consuming less food and by exercising more. I call this an elementary or ELEM program: *e*at *l*ess, *e*xercise *m*ore. I can also attempt to reduce my Type A behavior.

What is Type A behavior? This is behavior identified by two cardiologists, Dr. Meyer Friedman and Dr. Ray H. Rosenman, and believed to be a major cause of premature heart attacks. The most significant aspect of Type A behavior is a perpetual sense of time urgency or "hurry sickness." Persons engaging in Type A behavior are always setting deadlines for themselves and believe that they never have the time to complete the things they have programmed themselves to do. Type B behavior is characterized by feeling that there is sufficient time to complete all the things that need to be done.

Type A behavior is characterized by moving, walking, and eating very quickly, a tendency to speak rapidly, especially at the end of sentences, and an impatience and irritability with persons who do not operate at a rapid rate or at events that move too slowly. Type A behavior means trying to do or think of two or more things at the same time and saying you are sorry when you can't; it means feeling guilty when you relax; it means a *chronic sense of time urgency;* it means being preoccupied with getting the things worth *having* rather than trying to become the things worth *being;* it means valuing *achievement* ahead of *enjoyment.* Everything in life is seen as a challenge. Everything is competitively translated into numbers. Type B behavior is characterized by being free of the habits of Type A behavior, not suffering from a sense of time urgency and deadlines, being able to relax without feeling guilty, and being able to play for fun and relaxation. It means not needing to exhibit superiority, not feeling the need to display one's achievements and accomplishments unless this is demanded by the situation, and *not* harboring any free-floating hostility.

Friedman and Rosenman in their book *Type A Behavior and Your Heart* (Alfred A. Knopf, New York, 1974, and reprinted by Fawcett Crest Books as a paperback), which is based on research conducted in the late 1950s and 1960s, point out that when there is no Type A behavior pattern coronary heart disease rarely occurs before 70 years of age, independent of fatty foods eaten, smoking patterns, or the lack of exercise. When Type A behavior is characteristic coronary heart disease can easily occur when a person is in his 30s or 40s. Although Friedman and Rosenman have the term Type A *behavior* in the title of their book, they erroneously slip into taking about Type A *persons.* This can be misleading in that it implies a typology. No one exhibits Type A behavior in all situations nor does anyone exhibit Type B behavior in all situations. There is an interaction between the characteristics of the person and the situation. Some persons may exhibit Type A behavior in more situations than others, but some situations such as income tax filing date deadlines in April may call forth Type A behavior in almost all of us. Some persons may exhibit some facets of Type A behavior but not others. Although I have often been accused of doing two or more things at once, I certainly have fun and relax when I play, especially when I play tennis. I relax when I go to movies and plays. Therefore it is more useful to talk about Type A behavior or even Type A feelings and attitudes in specific situations than to talk about Type A persons.

The evidence is fairly compelling that Type A behavior greatly increases the probability of suffering from coronary disease. The aim should be to recognize the situations in which one engages in Type A behavior and to reduce or even possibly eliminate the intensity and frequency of Type A behavior in these situations.

During my depression I had a great deal of time to think about myself and my feelings and attitudes. I became aware of and confirmed what I had long suspected, namely, that I was engaging in a fair amount of Type A behavior. This was fully validated for me while I was convalescing from my heart attack. Although my affective disorder was primarily biochemical and physiological, my reactions were psychological and were to a great extent strongly influenced by my previous habits, experiences, and dynamics. When I was depressed, I was concerned because I wasn't working, that I wasn't doing the writing that I had planned to do, and felt guilty about not doing anything "useful." I became more compulsive than usual, more concerned about details. At times I was impulsive and everything had to be done immediately. This type of impulsiveness is probably related to Type A behavior. It would be interesting to determine whether Type A behavior is correlated with hypomanic behavior. To the best of my knowledge no one has investigated this hypothesis. One of the things I have learned as a result of my depression and heart attack is to pace myself. I probably don't do it so well and often as I should, but I probably haven't had enough practice at slowing down. I've had lots of practice at not pacing myself, at giving 150 percent effort, at working continuously without a rest, and at being a "workaholic." I have learned to say *No* to requests. I have learned to slow down.

It is important to learn to live with yourself and your resources, to know your own strengths and weaknesses. It is important to test out your abilities and your competencies. One of the first things that goes when you are depressed is your self-confidence. You become dependent and believe that you are no longer capable of doing anything well. During my sabbatical at Stanford University (1979–1980) I was on my own. This was the first time that I had been separated from my family for any length of time. I came to Stanford on my own for a variety of reasons. The basic reason was that my wife was getting tired of uprooting herself and traveling to live in strange towns or cities. It is always more difficult for the wife to adjust than for the husband. When our family spent my previous sabbatical year in Stockholm in 1973–1974 I went off to the university to work, the children went off to school, and Beatty was left with the job of coping with the house, the shopping, and a foreign language. We had spent four summers at the University of Illinois in Champaign-Urbana; we had gone on numerous trips, including the trip to Oxford. We live in a very comfortable house in Toronto and I guess Beatty had had enough of traveling. She did not want to uproot herself again; she wanted to stay put. I tried to persuade her to come but without success. Another factor was that our daughter was finishing her last year of high school during my sabbatical and it would not have been wise to transfer her to another school. My son was in the MBA program at York. So I went to Stanford by myself.

I had planned to leave for Stanford in the middle of September and to return to Ontario to present an invited address at the Ontario Symposium in Social Psychology being held at the University of Waterloo (60 miles west of Toronto), in the third week of October. Because of my heart attack I did not leave for Stanford until the end of October. I visited my family in Toronto at Christmas, at the end of February, at Easter (at the beginning of April), and returned permanently to Toronto and York University at the end of April. As a twenty-fifth wedding anniversary gift for my wife I presented her with a trip to Florence, for the two of us, from May 4 to May 22. (Our anniversary is June 26, but the climate in Florence is more suitable, that is, cooler, in May.) My wife is an artist and Florence was an ideal anniversary gift.

Although I was disappointed that my family was not coming with me to Stanford, in a sense I was secretly somewhat pleased. I had never really been on my own before. After my sophomore year at McGill University I went to Israel for a year, but with a group of others my own age, and we were usually three or four in a room. When I started the Ph.D. program at the University of Illinois I lived in a rooming house for the first year and shared a room with someone else. Then I got married. Except for the summers of 1964–1967, when I went off to Urbana for about three weeks in May, before the children finished school, and except for going to conferences and conventions, I had never really lived on my own before. Because my depression had temporarily made me doubt my own competence, I probably, unconsciously, wanted to prove that I could cope on my own.

It took me about 10 days to find a furnished apartment. Housing is difficult to come by in Palo Alto. After staying at a hotel for about two weeks I moved into a furnished studio apartment in downtown Palo Alto. The apartment was within walking distance of my office. The apartment manager lent me some blankets, pillows, and sheets and some friends lent me some dishes and towels. I bought some silverware. I cooked breakfast every day and usually made dinner about two or three times a week; nothing fancy, usually a steak or a frozen dinner. I found it a new and challenging experience to shop for groceries and to do the laundry. It was much easier than I expected. I suspect that what made it easier was the fact that I knew that it was a temporary arrangement.

Although I missed my family, I discovered an unanticipated fringe benefit of being on my own. That fringe benefit was privacy. The opportunity to be alone, to have time to think and to reflect, to come and go as I pleased and when I pleased, was something I really enjoyed. It's nice to be able to relax and to do as you please.

Now that I am back in Toronto I hope that I can maintain some of this privacy and quietness. Until my sabbatical year at Stanford I was always running around and always thrived on being with others— probably an example of Type A behavior. Perhaps the sabbatical has helped me move toward Type B behavior, part of which is being alone without deadlines. My wife and I discussed this sense of privacy when I visited Toronto during my sabbatical, and she said she appreciated it too. But then I guess she always has, so I don't believe that any changes in my attitude will create a problem in our relationship.

I accomplished a fair amount of work during my sabbatical. In addition to finishing a draft of this book, I started organizing the second edition of *Personality and Behavior Disorders* and have a draft for a chapter on interactional psychology. I was not exactly a monk; I visited a number of places in California, including San Francisco almost weekly, Sausalito, Yosemite Park, the Pacific coast, and Mendocino, which is north of San Francisco, Monterey, Carmel, and Santa Cruz, which is on the Pacific Coast south of San Francisco, and the wine country in the Napa Valley.

I am satisfied with my competence and self-confidence. I feel good about myself and know that my depression has taught me something about myself. I do not always have to run around trying to accomplish something. They also serve who only sit and think. Being is just as important as doing. Enjoyment is just as important as achievement. What useful advice can I provide to others who have been depressed?

Attention versus Memory

In earlier chapters (see especially Chapter 11) I mentioned that although depression may affect a person's attention there is no clear evidence that it directly affects memory. If you do not attend to something initially and it does not register, you obviously will not remember it later on. When a person is depressed he becomes self-preoccupied and therefore does not attend to the world about him. Therefore, later on, it may appear that he has a poor memory when in fact nothing registered for him to remember. There is no clear-cut evidence that unipolar ECT affects memory.

When I discussed this issue with a colleague I mentioned that I felt that my perceptions were dulled during my depression. He asked me if I had taken any notes in preparation for this book. I indicated that I had not and was writing all this from memory, about two and one-half years later. It may be therefore that not even my attention was affected during my depression, but rather by perception or appraisal or judgment of my surroundings had been distorted. Or perhaps the experiences were somehow registered at an unconscious level. Neither the depression nor the ECT produced any memory loss. I had a super memory before; I still have one now.

Recognizing the Symptoms of Depression

What are the symptoms of depression and how do you recognize them? Not everyone will have all of the symptoms, but these are the ones that are most characteristic, all of which were discussed in earlier chapters. If you have three or four of these symptoms and they persist for 10 days or more, run, don't walk to your doctor.

Depressed people feel hopeless, sad, and pessimistic. They have difficulty in sleeping, their sex drive is diminished, they are constantly tired, and they have difficulty concentrating. Many depressed people feel guilty, and all are indecisive and have low self-esteem. Anxiety and irritability are concomitants of depression and it is not unusual for the depressed person to have suicidal thoughts. Some frequent physical changes include dryness of the mouth, constipation, weight loss, nausea, and loss of appetite. Some of these symptoms also occur with other illnesses, but when they occur in a constellation or as a group it is fairly safe to assume that the person is depressed.

Seeking Help

How soon should one seek help? As soon as possible. If you think that you are depressed, see your family doctor or psychiatrist at once. It's better to be safe than sorry. Depression can be quite debilitating. If your illness is diagnosed as unipolar or bipolar depression, the best treatment is antidepressant drugs or ECT, supplemented by short-term counseling or psychotherapy. For a reactive or neurotic depression long-term psychotherapy plus antidepressants may be necessary. For a bipolar or unipolar depression psychotherapy or psychoanalysis without antide-pressants or ECT may not be effective. If you are really depressed, you cannot engage in a meaningful psychotherapeutic exchange. (Dr. Silvano Arieti, a psychoanalytically oriented psychiatrist, believes that cognitively oriented psychotherapy alone can be an effective treatment in severe depression.) Remember that it takes two or three weeks for the antidepressants to have their therapeutic effect. Depression can remit spontaneously but one should always seek a consultation if an episode has occurred.

The Role of the Family

The role of the family is a crucial one, both before you start and during treatment. Often a depressed person may not be in a position to decide that help is needed, in which case the guidance of a spouse, parent, or significant other should be followed. During the treatment you need your family for physical and emotional support. If you are really depressed you cannot cope with day-to-day living by yourself. It is not possible to have ECT on an outpatient basis without family support. Many need hospitalization because there is no one to look after them; they have no family support. Often during an emotional illness family conflicts may become exacerbated. In many cases the family becomes more closely knit. I would not have survived without the assistance of my family.

Depression is a common pervasive illness affecting all social classes, but it is eminently treatable. A great deal of heartbreak can be avoided by early detection and treatment. There is nothing to be ashamed of. There is no stigma attached to having an affective disorder. It is unwise to try to hide it and not to seek help. I lived to tell my tale and to write about it.

Afterword

At this writing in mid-April 1981 I have been symptom-free for almost three years. As in April 1980 and April 1979, I am *not* experiencing an emotional crisis and I hope I never do again. I feel in excellent health both emotionally and physically. The lithium treatment is being stopped on a trial basis, but, I know that lithium is available to me if I need it again. This in itself is reassuring.

I am reminded of a telephone conversation I had with my wife just one year ago, in mid-April 1980. I had phoned from Stanford to speak with her in Toronto and I mentioned that I had to do a lot of work to finish the first draft of Chapter 12, the last chapter in this book, before I left Stanford at the end of the month. Beatty said to me, "What's so terrible if you don't finish?" That put it all in perspective for me. I intend to live life to the fullest, but carefully. The sun will rise and shine whether or not I finish things today. But it's nice knowing that I did finish the first draft of this book before I left Stanford!

T H E   E N D

(Actually, the Beginning)